LEADER

THE BIBLE YEAR

A Journey Through Scripture in 365 Days

MAGREY R. DEVEGA

Abingdon Press | Nashville

THE BIBLE YEAR
A Journey Through Scripture in 365 Days
Leader Guide

Copyright © 2021 Abingdon Press
All rights reserved.

No part of this work may be reproduced or transmitted in any form or by any means, electronic or mechanical, including photocopying and recording, or by any information storage or retrieval system, except as may be expressly permitted by the 1976 Copyright Act, the 1998 Digital Millennium Copyright Act, or in writing from the publisher. Requests for permission can be addressed to Rights and Permissions, The United Methodist Publishing House, 2222 Rosa L. Parks Blvd., Nashville, TN 37228-1306 or e-mailed to permissions@abingdonpress.com.

978-1-7910-2343-0

Scripture quotations unless noted otherwise are from the Common English Bible. Copyright © 2011 by the Common English Bible. All rights reserved. Used by permission. www.CommonEnglishBible.com.

21 22 23 24 25 26 27 28 29 30 — 10 9 8 7 6 5 4 3 2 1
MANUFACTURED IN THE UNITED STATES OF AMERICA

Contents

To the Leader 9

Session 1: Genesis 1:1–11:32 15

Session 2: Genesis 12:1–30:43 18

Session 3: Genesis 31:1–Exodus 12:30 21

Session 4: Exodus 12:31–34:35 24

Session 5: Exodus 35:1–Leviticus 23:44 27

Session 6: Leviticus 24:1–Numbers 21:35 30

Session 7: Numbers 22:1–Deuteronomy 16:22 33

Session 8: Deuteronomy 17:1–Joshua 11:23 36

Session 9: Joshua 12:1–Judges 16:31 39

Session 10: Judges 17:1–1 Samuel 15:35 42

Session 11: 1 Samuel 16:1–2 Samuel 7:29 45

Session 12: 2 Samuel 8:1–1 Kings 11:43 48

Session 13: 1 Kings 12:1–2 Kings 17:41 51

Session 14: 2 Kings 18:1–1 Chronicles 27:34 54

Session 15: 1 Chronicles 28:1–2 Chronicles 24:27.................... 57

Session 16: 2 Chronicles 25:1–Nehemiah 4:23....................... 60

Session 17: Nehemiah 5:1–Job 14:22................................. 63

Session 18: Job 15:1–Psalm 12:8.................................... 66

Session 19: Psalms 13:1–41:13 69

Session 20: Psalms 42:1–68:35 72

Session 21: Psalms 69:1–101:8 75

Session 22: Psalms 102:1–126:6 78

Session 23: Psalm 127:1–Proverbs 3:35.............................. 81

Session 24: Proverbs 4:1–15:33..................................... 84

Session 25: Proverbs 16:1–26:28.................................... 87

Session 26: Proverbs 27:1–Ecclesiastes 12:14........................ 90

Session 27: Song of Solomon 1:1–Isaiah 23:18 93

Session 28: Isaiah 24:1–52:12 96

Session 29: Isaiah 52:13–Jeremiah 16:21............................ 99

Session 30: Jeremiah 17:1–49:39................................... 102

Session 31: Jeremiah 50:1–Ezekiel 21:32............................ 105

Session 32: Ezekiel 22:1–Daniel 6:28............................... 108

Session 33: Daniel 7:1–Amos 9:15 111

Session 34: Obadiah–Habakkuk 3:19 114

Session 35: Zephaniah 1:1–Malachi 4:6............................. 117

Session 36: Matthew 1:1–12:50 120

Session 37: Matthew 13:1–25:46 123

Session 38 Matthew 26:1–Mark 10:45 126

Session 39: Mark 10:46–Luke 4:13 129

Session 40: Luke 4:14–14:35 132

Session 41: Luke 15:1–24:53 135

Session 42: John 1:1–10:42 138

Session 43: John 11:1–Acts 5:16 141

Session 44: Acts 5:17–23:35 144

Session 45: Acts 24:1–Romans 13:14 147

Session 46: Romans 14:1–2 Corinthians 3:18 150

Session 47: 2 Corinthians 4:1–Ephesians 2:22 153

Session 48: Ephesians 3:1–1 Thessalonians 3:13 156

Session 49: 1 Thessalonians 4:1–Titus 3:15 159

Session 50: Philemon–James 2:26 162

Session 51: James 3:1–1 John 5:21 165

Session 52: 2 John–Revelation 11:19 168

Session 53: Revelation 12:1–22:21 171

Notes 175

AMPLIFY® MEDIA

Enrich your small group experience with weekly videos for *The Bible Year*, available through Amplify Media.

Use **Promo Code BibleYear22** to get
3 months free if you sign up for a 1-year subscription.*
Or call 800-672-1789 to ask about our latest offer.

Amplify Media is a multi-media platform that delivers high quality, searchable content with an emphasis on Wesleyan perspectives for church-wide, group, or individual use on any device at any time. In a world of sometimes overwhelming choices, Amplify gives church leaders media capabilities that are contemporary, relevant, effective and, most importantly, affordable and sustainable.

With Amplify Media you can:

- Provide a reliable source of Christian content through a Wesleyan lens for teaching, training, and inspiration in a customizable library,
- Deliver your own preaching and worship content in a way your congregation knows and appreciates,
- Build your church's capacity to innovate with engaging content and accessible technology,
- Equip your congregation to better understand the Bible and its application, and
- Deepen discipleship beyond the church walls.

Sign up for Amplify Media at:
https://www.amplifymedia.com/annual-pricing.
*Use **Promo Code BibleYear22** at checkout.**

**Promo code valid from October 1, 2021 through April 30, 2022.*
After promo code expires, call 800-672-1789 to ask about our latest offer.

To the Leader

Reading the Bible promises to enrich our faith, as we find ourselves in its stories and teachings and encounter the God who created us and called us to be followers of Jesus. Reading the Bible together with others—whether we do so as a small group or as a whole congregation—draws us closer to God and to one another. When we read in conversation with others, it opens a path for us to ask and wrestle with difficult questions we have about Scripture, or that the Bible poses to us. Often, it is the mere freedom and permission to raise questions aloud with others that can encourage people who would otherwise struggle with the faith. Most importantly, reading the Bible together can elicit novel insights from the diversity of voices around the room, unlocking new, life-giving ways to look at a text.

This Leader Guide contains a year's worth of small group sessions to help you guide your small group in reading the Bible together, using *The Bible Year* as a resource. Whether you commit to reading the whole Bible together in a year, or choose a portion of it, this resource will help you dig deeper into the text and its meaning for your life. As you read and lead your group's discussions, may the Holy Spirit speak to you and guide you to encounter God each time you open the Bible and each time you gather together.

How to Facilitate This Study

This study makes use of the following components:

- **The Bible.** A variety of translations are both allowable and desirable in your small group. Multiple translations allow you to compare wording and open the possibility for new insights into the text. Some great translations include the Common English Bible (CEB), New Revised Standard Version (NRSV), and New International Version (NIV).

- The daily devotional, *The Bible Year: A Journey Through Scripture in 365 Days*. The overviews and daily devotions give you and your group background and prompt reflection on your daily Bible reading. The devotional includes space to write down your thoughts briefly each day.
- This **Leader Guide.**
- *The Bible Year* videos (optional), available via Amplify Media (www.amplifymedia.com). There are fifty-three short videos available, featuring Magrey deVega and other pastors, scholars, and Bible teachers exploring the text and setting the stage for group discussion. If you choose to use *The Bible Year* videos, you will need a computer or television with Internet access so that you can watch the video segments as part of your group session.

Each session should take approximately 45–60 minutes to complete, and consists of the following segments:

- **Opening (5–15 minutes):** Open with prayer, review the Scripture texts, and invite initial impressions and responses from the daily devotional.
- **Discussion (30–45 minutes):** Discuss the Scripture text using discussion questions that are provided.
- **Closing (5 minutes):** Invite the group to raise any prayer concerns or reasons for thanksgiving, then close with prayer.

HELPFUL HINTS

Preparing for Each Session

- Pray for wisdom and discernment from the Holy Spirit, for you and for each member of the group, as you prepare for the study.

To the Leader

- Before each session, familiarize yourself with the Scripture passages. Read the text carefully and make notes of anything you want to be sure to discuss.
- Review the discussion questions for the session and select the ones you want to spend the most time with in your group. Be prepared, however, to adjust the session as group members interact and as questions arise. Prepare carefully, but allow space for the Holy Spirit to move in and through the group members and through you as facilitator.
- Prepare the space where the group will meet so that the space will enhance the learning process. Ideally, group members should be seated around a table or in a circle so that all can see one another.

Shaping the Learning Environment

- Create a climate of openness, encouraging group members to participate as they feel comfortable.
- Remember that some people will jump right in with answers and comments, while others need time to process what is being discussed.
- If you notice that some group members seem never to be able to enter the conversation, ask them if they have thoughts to share. Give everyone a chance to talk, but keep the conversation moving. Moderate to prevent a few individuals from doing all the talking.
- Communicate the importance of group discussions and group exercises.
- If no one answers at first during discussions, do not be afraid of silence. Count silently to ten, then say something such as, "Would anyone like to go first?" If no one responds, venture an answer yourself and ask for comments.
- Model openness as you share with the group. Group members will follow your example. If you limit your sharing to a surface level, others will follow suit.

- Encourage multiple answers or responses before moving on to the next question.
- **Ask:** "Why?" or "Why do you believe that?" or "Can you say more about that?" to help continue a discussion and give it greater depth.
- Affirm others' responses with comments such as "Great" or "Thanks" or "Good insight"—especially if it's the first time someone has spoken during the group session.
- Monitor your own contributions. If you are doing most of the talking, back off so that you do not train the group to listen rather than speak up.
- Remember that you do not have to have all the answers. Your job is to keep the discussion going and encourage participation.

Managing the Session

- Honor the time schedule. If a session is running longer than expected, get consensus from the group before continuing beyond the agreed-upon ending time.
- Involve group members in various aspects of the group session, such as saying prayers or reading the Scripture.
- As always in discussions that may involve personal sharing, confidentiality is essential. Group members should never pass along stories that have been shared in the group. Remind the group members at each session: confidentiality is crucial to the success of this study.

TIPS FOR ONLINE MEETINGS

Meeting online is a great option for a number of situations. During a time of a public-health hazard, such as the COVID-19 pandemic, online meetings are a welcome opportunity for folks to converse while seeing each other's faces. Online meetings can also expand the "neighborhood" of possible group members, because people can log in from just about anywhere in the world. This also gives those who do not have access to transportation or who prefer not to travel at certain times of day the chance to participate.

There are a number of platforms for online meetings. Google has two products, one called Google Hangouts and one called Google Meet. You need only a Google account to use them, which is free.

Another popular option is Zoom. This platform is used quite a bit by businesses. If your church has an account, this can be a good medium. Individuals can obtain free accounts, but those offer meetings of no longer than 40 minutes. For longer meetings (which you will want for this study), you must pay for an account.

Some other platforms to consider: GoToMeeting, Web Meeting, Microsoft Teams, and others. Search the internet for "web conferencing software," and you will probably find a link to top-ten rating sites that can help you choose.

Training and Practice

- Choose a platform and practice using it, so you are comfortable with it. Engage in a couple of practice runs with another person.
- Set up a training meeting.
- In advance, teach participants how to log in. Tell them that you will send them an invitation via email, and that it will include a link for them to click at the time of the meeting.
- For those who do not have internet service, let them know they may telephone into the meeting. Provide them the number and let them know that there is usually a unique phone number for each meeting.
- During the training meeting, show participants the basic tools available for them to use. They can learn other tools as they feel more confident.

During the Meetings

- **Early invitations.** Send out invitations at least a week in advance. Many meeting platforms enable you to do this through their software.
- **Early log in.** Participants should log in at least ten minutes in advance, to test their audio and their video connections.
- **Talking/not talking.** Instruct participants to keep their microphones muted during the meeting, so extraneous noise from their location does not interrupt the meeting. This includes chewing or yawning sounds, which can be embarrassing! When it is time for discussion, participants can unmute themselves. However, ask them to raise their hand or wave when they are ready to share, so you can call on them. Give folks a few minutes to speak up. They may not be used to conversing in web conferences.

SESSION 1

Genesis 1:1–11:32

Overview

In the opening chapters of Genesis, God creates the heavens and the earth. God makes humans in God's image, entrusting them with dominion over all other creatures and charging them to care for the earth.

When the first man and woman follow the cunning serpent's suggestion and eat fruit God had forbidden them to eat, they try in vain to hide from God. God drives them out of the garden of Eden into a life of hard labor and broken relationships with nature, each other, and God.

As humanity grows, so does its violence and wickedness, beginning when Cain murders his brother, Abel. God destroys the world with a great flood, but first directs Noah, a righteous man, to build a large boat in which he, his family, and some of every living species survive. God establishes a covenant—a solemn agreement—with Noah and all living creatures, and promises to never destroy the world by water again.

The world's nations descend from Noah. When they try to build a tower that reaches the heavens, God confuses their shared language and scatters them across the world.

Opening

+ Begin with prayer.

- Invite a volunteer or volunteers to summarize the week's readings, using the overview above as a reference.
- Invite the group to share initial responses to the readings, as well as any questions they may have.
- Ask for volunteers to share some of their daily responses from this week from *The Bible Year* devotional.
- If you are using *The Bible Year* videos, play the video for today's session now.
- Continue your discussion of the week's Bible passages with the questions below.

Discussion Questions

1. Genesis contains two stories about God creating the world (1:1–2:4a; 2:4b–3:24). Why? How do these accounts contradict and complement each other? What questions about the world's and humanity's origins do they leave unanswered?
2. What does the Bible's assertion that God is Creator mean to you personally?
3. Genesis 1 emphasizes God saw creation as "supremely good" (v. 31). Where do you see this fundamental goodness in the world? Where is it harder to see, and why? How are you drawing attention to the world's goodness?
4. If humans are created in God's image (1:27), what does this truth mean for the way we should relate to the created world, to other life, to each other, and to God? Give specific examples.
5. Why did God command the man and woman to not eat from "the tree of the knowledge of good and evil" (2:17)? Why did they? What changes after they do?
6. How does the primal drama of disobedience and its consequences in Genesis 2–3 play out in the world today? In your life?

Genesis 1:1–11:32

7. Why does Cain kill Abel (4:1-16)? What does the story of the world's first murder tell us about human beings? What does it tell us about God? Where do you hear innocent blood crying for justice today? How, specifically, are you acting as your brothers' and sisters' keepers?
8. What does the story of Noah's Ark tell us about how God regards and responds to human violence? Why does the covenant between God and "every living thing…on behalf of every future generation" (9:12) matter today?
9. Why does God stop the people from building their tower (11:1-9)? What do you think about this story's explanation of humanity's linguistic and geographic diversity as an act of God? Are humans still trying to build such towers today? If so, how?

Closing

- Ask for several volunteers to summarize what they have found most meaningful about your discussion or about the biblical text this week. How might God be calling them to respond to it?
- Invite the group to raise any prayer concerns or lift up any reasons for joy and thanksgiving.
- Lead the group in a short closing prayer or invite a volunteer to do so.

Gen 1: – Dicotomy vs spectrum

SESSION 2

Genesis 12:1–30:43

Overview

God tells Abram to travel to a new land God will show him. God promises to make Abram father of a large nation, one family through whom all families of the earth will be blessed. God later repeats this promise in a formal covenant signified by male circumcision. Abram (Abraham) and his wife Sarai (Sarah) obey the call and—after a sojourn in Egypt, where the pharaoh takes Sarah for himself for a time—settle in the land of Canaan.

After leaving Egypt, Abraham fathers a son named Ishmael with Hagar, an Egyptian girl enslaved to Sarah. After Sarah bears a son named Isaac in her old age, she sends Hagar and Ishmael away. God promises to make a great nation of Ishmael, but Isaac is the son through whom God will fulfill the promise to Abraham.

God tests Abraham, commanding him to sacrifice Isaac. God stops the sacrifice at the last possible moment, and Abraham sacrifices a ram instead.

Isaac marries Rebekah. Their twin sons, Esau and Jacob, struggle with each other from conception. Jacob ultimately cheats Esau out of the birthright and their father's blessing. Fleeing from his brother, Jacob has a dream in which God reaffirms for him the promise made to Abraham and to Isaac.

Genesis 12:1–30:43

While away from home, Jacob works for his uncle Laban, who tricks Jacob into marrying Laban's daughter Leah before marrying Rachel, the woman Jacob loves.

Opening

- Begin with prayer.
- Invite a volunteer or volunteers to summarize the week's readings, using the overview above as a reference.
- Invite the group to share initial responses to the readings, as well as any questions they may have.
- Ask for volunteers to share some of their daily responses from this week from *The Bible Year* devotional.
- If you are using *The Bible Year* videos, play the video for today's session now.
- Continue your discussion of the week's Bible passages with the questions below.

Discussion Questions

1. What does God promise Abraham (12:1-3)? Why? How many ways is God's promise threatened in this week's stories? Have apparent threats to God's promises ever made you worried or afraid? How might these stories help you or others deal with such worries and fears?
2. Briefly describe each of the characters in this week's stories: Abraham, Sarah, Hagar, Rebekah, Esau, Jacob, Laban. Do you recognize yourself in these characters? With whom do you identify most closely?
3. What do the stories of these individuals in Genesis tell us about God's willingness and ability to work with and through human beings?
4. Sarah and Abraham make their own plans for bringing about God's promise (16:1-16; 21:8-21). What happens? When and how, if ever, have you taken it

The Bible Year: Leader Guide

upon yourself to hurry God's future along? What happened?

5. Islam regards Ishmael as an important patriarch and prophet. In the New Testament, Paul calls those who believe in Jesus the children of Abraham. What does Abraham's significance for Jews, Christians, and Muslims suggest about how the three "Abrahamic religions" should relate to each other, globally and in your own community?

6. Why does God command Abraham to sacrifice Isaac (22:1-19)? Was Abraham right to obey? Why or why not? Has God ever asked a great sacrifice of you? What did you do? Would you do the same thing again?

7. The stories of Jacob tricking Esau (25:29-34; 27:1-45) and of Laban tricking Jacob (29:15-30) show the family through whom God decided to bring blessing was not perfect. What are your most pressing concerns about your family? What do you do about them? How do you entrust them and your family to God?

Closing

- Ask for several volunteers to summarize what they have found most meaningful about your discussion or about the biblical text this week. How might God be calling them to respond to it?
- Invite the group to raise any prayer concerns or lift up any reasons for joy and thanksgiving.
- Lead the group in a short closing prayer or invite a volunteer to do so.

SESSION 3

Genesis 31:1– Exodus 12:30

Overview

A prosperous Jacob returns to Canaan. The night before he reunites and is reconciled with his brother, Esau, he wrestles with a mysterious man who renames him Israel, "because you struggled with God and with men and won."

When Jacob's son Joseph dreams he will rise to greatness, his envious brothers sell him into slavery. As a slave in Egypt, Joseph's gift for interpreting dreams and skill in planning lead to his appointment as Pharaoh's highest official.

When famine strikes Egypt and surrounding lands, Joseph's grain distribution plan saves many lives—including those of his brothers, who come to Egypt for food. After Joseph reveals himself to his brothers and forgives them, they come with Jacob to live in Egypt.

In time, a new pharaoh, afraid of his country's Israelite (Hebrew) population, enslaves them and tries to kill their baby boys. One Hebrew baby who survives is Moses. Through him, God will free the Israelites.

When Pharaoh will not let the Israelites go as Moses demands, God unleashes ten terrible plagues, culminating in the death of all Egyptian firstborn people and animals. God commands the Israelites to eat a special meal on the night of the last plague, marking their doors with a lamb's blood so that death will pass over them.

Opening

- Begin with prayer.
- Invite a volunteer or volunteers to summarize the week's readings, using the overview above as a reference.
- Invite the group to share initial responses to the readings, as well as any questions they may have.
- Ask for volunteers to share some of their daily responses from this week from *The Bible Year* devotional.
- If you are using *The Bible Year* videos, play the video for today's session now.
- Continue your discussion of the week's Bible passages with the questions below.

Discussion Questions

1. The story of Joseph (Genesis 37–50) reads as enjoyably as a modern novella thanks to its complex plot, use of suspense and irony, and characterization. What do you like or dislike about Joseph's story? What stories from your own or others' lives could you tell about God bringing good out of what others intended for evil?
2. What reasons are given for Joseph's brothers hating him? How would you characterize the relationships in Jacob's family? What changes do you see as the story progresses? What is the source of these changes?
3. What do the stories about Dinah's rape (Genesis 34) and Tamar's plan to get justice from Judah (Genesis 38) tell us about women in ancient Israel? How, do they address issues of sex and sexual violence, men and women's relationships, and power in our society? Where is God in these stories?

Genesis 31:1–Exodus 12:30

 4. In Exodus 1, why does the pharaoh fear the Israelites? Had he known (or chosen to remember) Joseph's part in Egypt's history, would he have been afraid? Why or why not? How do the pharaoh's fears persist in societies today?

5. Notice the people in Exodus 1 and 2 who work against Pharaoh. What common threads link them together?

6. In Exodus 3, what does God's name, "I AM," tell us about who God is and what God does? For an ancient society where knowing someone's name was believed to give you power over them, how would God's name reflect God's freedom? How is God's name good news for you? For your congregation? For your community?

7. The Exodus story repeatedly says the pharaoh refused to free the Israelites both because he changed his mind and because God hardened his heart. How do these explanations contradict or complement each other? What does this story tell us about human sin and God's authority?

8. God instructs the Israelites to celebrate the Passover meal as a perpetual reminder of how God freed them from slavery (Exodus 12:1-28). How does your community remember and celebrate what God has done? How do you do so in your life?

Closing

- Ask for several volunteers to summarize what they have found most meaningful about your discussion or about the biblical text this week. How might God be calling them to respond to it?
- Invite the group to raise any prayer concerns or lift up any reasons for joy and thanksgiving.
- Lead the group in a short closing prayer or invite a volunteer to do so.

SESSION 4

Exodus 12:31–34:35

Overview

Preceding them in a pillar of cloud by day and of fire by night, God leads the Israelites out of Egypt, bringing them safely through the Red Sea but drowning the Egyptians who attempt to pursue them through its waters.

Three thirst-filled days later, the Israelites begin what will become a familiar pattern of complaining to Moses, who complains to God, who meets the people's needs. God turns bitter waters sweet and brings water out of a rock. God sends quails and miraculous bread from heaven—the people call it manna, which means, What is it?

The Israelites reach Mount Sinai. God descends on the mountain in fire and cloud and claims the Israelites as God's own people, chosen to live as a holy nation. God makes a covenant with the Israelites and gives them laws, including the Ten Commandments, which the people promise to obey. God then gives Moses instructions for building the Tabernacle, the ark of the covenant, and the other instruments of worship.

But while Moses spends forty days and nights on Sinai receiving this covenant's terms from God, the people ask Moses's brother, Aaron, to make them an idol they can worship, which Aaron does. When Moses discovers the people celebrating the golden calf, he angrily breaks the

Exodus 12:31–34:35

stone tablets on which God had written the covenant and punishes the people. God commands Moses to make new tablets on which to write God's renewal of the covenant.

Opening

- Begin with prayer.
- Invite a volunteer or volunteers to summarize the week's readings, using the overview above as a reference.
- Invite the group to share initial responses to the readings, as well as any questions they may have.
- Ask for volunteers to share some of their daily responses from this week from *The Bible Year* devotional.
- If you are using *The Bible Year* videos, play the video for today's session now.
- Continue your discussion of the week's Bible passages with the questions below.

Discussion Questions

1. The song Moses and his sister Miriam lead the Israelites in singing at the Red Sea (Exodus 15:1-21) describes God as a warrior. How can this song shape God's people's attitudes and actions today when we see the powerful plotting against the powerless (v. 9)?
2. How has God sustained your congregation or you personally through difficult times as God sustained the Israelites? Who in your community needs bread, and how is God providing it to them through you?
3. At Mount Sinai, God identifies Israel as "a kingdom of priests for me and a holy nation" (19:5-6). What does this identity mean? How does this calling relate to the promise God made to Abraham in Genesis 12:1-3? Is "chosen" status a privilege or a responsibility—or both—and why?

4. The Ten Commandments (20:1-17) are a small portion of the law God gives in this week's chapters. Are they more important than the other commandments? Why or why not? To what extent are they specific to Israel's history with God, and to what extent are they universally applicable?
5. Why do worship matters like festivals, the Tabernacle, and the priesthood receive such detailed attention in this week's chapters? What does the way a community worships God reveal about its priorities, values, and commitments?
6. How do you react to the punishments Moses metes out for the people's idolatry (32:19-20, 25-29)? What are the "golden calves" we as a society and you personally are tempted to dance around today? What punishment or consequences might we receive?
7. What is God's name according to 34:5-7? How could these verses help us interpret God's name in Exodus 3:14?

Closing

- Ask for several volunteers to summarize what they have found most meaningful about your discussion or about the biblical text this week. How might God be calling them to respond to it?
- Invite the group to raise any prayer concerns or lift up any reasons for joy and thanksgiving.
- Lead the group in a short closing prayer or invite a volunteer to do so.

SESSION 5

Exodus 35:1– Leviticus 23:44

Overview

Artisans and craftspeople among the Israelites construct the Tabernacle according to God's specifications. This large, elaborately furnished tent is where God's presence dwells among the Israelites. It contains the ark of the covenant, the box holding the tablets of God's law, topped by a cover—sometimes called the "mercy seat"—with carved cherubim on top. The ark is a symbol of God's presence in the Tabernacle.

Aaron and his sons serve as priests, making offerings and animal sacrifices in the Tabernacle. The Book of Leviticus details their duties, but much of the book addresses all Israelites. It draws distinctions between what foods, animals, and personal conditions are clean and unclean, pure and impure—which are acceptable in God's sight and which are not. In observing the distinction between these categories in their lives, the Israelites answer their calling to be God's holy people.

Leviticus also describes how the Israelites should observe several holy days and festivals, including the Day of Reconciliation or Day of Atonement. On that day, the priests sacrifice a bull for their own sin and a goat for the people's. They also confess the people's sins over the head of a live goat before it is sent into the wilderness, taking the people's sins with it.

Opening

- Begin with prayer.
- Invite a volunteer or volunteers to summarize the week's readings, using the overview above as a reference.
- Invite the group to share initial responses to the readings, as well as any questions they may have.
- Ask for volunteers to share some of their daily responses from this week from *The Bible Year* devotional.
- If you are using *The Bible Year* videos, play the video for today's session now.
- Continue your discussion of the week's Bible passages with the questions below.

Discussion Questions

1. What does the level of detail with which Exodus describes the Tabernacle and its furnishings (25:1–31:11; 35:4–39:31) suggest about the structure's purpose and significance?
2. What does the Tabernacle's construction suggest about the role artists and craftspeople such as Bezalel and Oholiab (35:30–36:7) can and do play in the community of faith?
3. What places in your life, past or present, do you consider holy, and why?
4. Leviticus is largely a book about ritual. How do rituals shape a community and keep it together? How do rituals teach or reinforce morality?
5. What are some of the most important rituals, religious or otherwise, you have observed or still observe? How do we know when our communities need new rituals?

6. God tells Aaron to "distinguish between the holy and the common, and between the unclean and the clean" (Leviticus 10:10). Why does this distinction matter so much, even costing Nadab and Abihu their lives when they ignore it (10:1-2)? How sharp a distinction do you draw between holy and common in your life, and why?
7. How do you react to the purification laws in Leviticus 12–15? What was their intent in ancient Israel? Do they offer anything of value to Christians today? If so, what? If not, why not?
8. Leviticus 19 shows us being holy is about more than performing rituals. Which of this chapter's ethical concerns do you think remain most urgent today, and why? Which of its moral demands do you find most challenging?

Closing

- Ask for several volunteers to summarize what they have found most meaningful about your discussion or about the biblical text this week. How might God be calling them to respond to it?
- Invite the group to raise any prayer concerns or lift up any reasons for joy and thanksgiving.
- Lead the group in a short closing prayer or invite a volunteer to do so.

SESSION 6

Leviticus 24:1– Numbers 21:35

Overview

Among the remaining commandments in Leviticus, God instructs the Israelites to observe every seventh year as a sabbath year, during which the land rests from growing crops; and every fiftieth year as a jubilee year in which Israelites return to lands they had to sell and indentured servants return to their families.

Numbers begins with a census of the Israelites. After a year at Mount Sinai, the people resume their journey to Canaan. They also resume their complaints, fondly remembering the food they ate in Egypt. When Moses complains to God about his burden as leader, God instructs him to appoint seventy elders to help.

But controversy continues. Moses's siblings, Aaron and Miriam, express envy of Moses's primacy. God punishes Miriam with diseased skin. She is put out of the camp, unclean, for a week.

Spies spend forty days scouting Canaan. They return with a huge cluster of grapes, evidence of the land's bounty. But most of the spies despair of the Israelites' ability to conquer the land. Only Caleb and Joshua encourage trust in God's promise. When the people want to return to Egypt, God threatens to strike them with plague and raise up a greater nation from Moses alone. Moses successfully intercedes for them, but God swears this generation will not enter the Promised Land. Neither shall Moses, because at Meribah he fails to glorify God for miraculously given water. The Israelites will wander in the wilderness for forty years before they enter the Promised Land.

Opening

- Begin with prayer.
- Invite a volunteer or volunteers to summarize the week's readings, using the overview above as a reference.
- Invite the group to share initial responses to the readings, as well as any questions they may have.
- Ask for volunteers to share some of their daily responses from this week from *The Bible Year* devotional.
- If you are using *The Bible Year* videos, play the video for today's session now.
- Continue your discussion of the week's Bible passages with the questions below.

Discussion Questions

1. How easy or difficult would it be for our society to observe jubilees in which debts were forgiven and inequities addressed (Leviticus 25)? How might the practice benefit society?
2. How can the church observe jubilee-like practices in its own life? How can people of faith remind the world we are all "just immigrants and foreign guests" on God's earth (25:23)?
3. God tells Moses to select seventy elders to help him lead Israel (Numbers 11:16-17; compare Exodus 18:13-26, in which Moses' father-in-law makes the same suggestion). How is leadership shared in your church? How would you improve your church's

leadership model if you could, and why? Who are the people outside of formal leadership—the "Eldads and Medads" (11:26-29)—who have prophetic words your church needs to hear?

4. Why doesn't Aaron suffer the same punishment as Miriam for speaking against Moses (12:1-16)? When, if ever, is it not only permissible but faithful to speak against religious and spiritual leaders?

5. Why does the people's acceptance of the spies' majority report about Canaan so provoke God's anger (14:11-12)? How does Moses persuade God not to destroy them (14:13-19)? Is God's decision to not allow this generation into the Promised Land gracious? Why or why not?

6. Scripture says between Korah and his men's rebellion (16:1-35) and the plague following the rebellion of "the whole congregation" (16:41-49), some fifteen thousand Israelites die. Why did Israel remember these stories of rebellion? How can we remember the stories of our churches' and our own spiritual rebellions and failures in healthy and constructive ways?

Closing

+ Ask for several volunteers to summarize what they have found most meaningful about your discussion or about the biblical text this week. How might God be calling them to respond to it?
+ Invite the group to raise any prayer concerns or lift up any reasons for joy and thanksgiving.
+ Lead the group in a short closing prayer or invite a volunteer to do so.

SESSION 7

Numbers 22:1– Deuteronomy 16:22

Overview

As the Israelites draw closer to Canaan, King Balak of Moab hires the prophet Balaam to come and curse them. An angel from God, visible only to Balaam's donkey, blocks Balaam's way—and the donkey gives his rider a divinely enabled rebuke when Balaam beats him for refusing to go on. God allows Balaam to go to Moab, but the prophet is able to speak only words of blessing on God's people.

From a mountaintop, God shows Moses the Promised Land he will not be allowed to enter. Moses ordains Joshua as his successor. In the meantime, he continues to lead the people, including to successful war against and plunder of the Midianites. God gives instructions for the conquest and division of Canaan to come.

In Deuteronomy, Moses reviews for the Israelites the story of their journey from Mount Horeb (another name for Mount Sinai) and repeats the law God has given them. More than a bare repetition, Moses's extended speech in Deuteronomy stresses the Israelites' need to obey God's law once they settle in the Promised Land. Faithful obedience to God's covenant will bring blessing and prosperity; disobedience—

especially in the forms of idolatry, intermingling with Canaanites, and social injustice—will bring disaster and dispossession.

Opening

- Begin with prayer.
- Invite a volunteer or volunteers to summarize the week's readings, using the overview above as a reference.
- Invite the group to share initial responses to the readings, as well as any questions they may have.
- Ask for volunteers to share some of their daily responses from this week from *The Bible Year* devotional.
- If you are using *The Bible Year* videos, play the video for today's session now.
- Continue your discussion of the week's Bible passages with the questions below.

Discussion Questions

1. How does the story of Balaam (Numbers 22–24) highlight God's care for the Israelites? When and how has God spoken to you in surprising ways—even if not as surprising as through a donkey?
2. Have you ever felt God moving or even compelling you to speak words you hadn't planned or didn't want to speak? What happened?
3. What problem do Zelophehad's daughters face (Numbers 27:1-12)? How does the community solve the problem? What does this story (continued in 36:1-12) suggest about how God's people know when its rules and traditions need to change, and how to go about changing them?
4. God orders the Israelites to drive out Canaan's inhabitants when they enter the land (Numbers 33:50-56), and this week's chapters contain stories about Israel's violence against non-Israelites (for instance, Numbers

25:1-18; 31:1-54). They will not be the last such stories we read this year. Do you believe God commanded this violence? Why or why not? What value, if any, do these stories have for Jews and Christians today?
5. Deuteronomy is written as a long speech in which Moses reviews Israel's journey to Canaan. Why does Moses give this speech at this moment? When has your congregation, or when have you personally, benefited from hearing someone else review your history with God, and how?
6. Deuteronomy 6:4-5 remains a core Jewish confession of faith, the Shema (Hebrew for "hear"). What does it mean, practically, to love God with all one's heart, being, and strength? How does your congregation keep its confession of faith front and center? How does it communicate that faith to its children?
7. When, if ever, has your congregation or have you been tempted to forget God in good times (Deuteronomy 8:11-20)? What has happened in such times to keep you faithful?

Closing

- Ask for several volunteers to summarize what they have found most meaningful about your discussion or about the biblical text this week. How might God be calling them to respond to it?
- Invite the group to raise any prayer concerns or lift up any reasons for joy and thanksgiving.
- Lead the group in a short closing prayer or invite a volunteer to do so.

SESSION 8

Deuteronomy 17:1– Joshua 11:23

Overview

Moses teaches Israel about the roles of priests and judges, warns them of the limits on power their future kings must respect, and tells them to look for God to raise up a prophet like him. He repeats God's blessings for obedience and curses for disobedience and leads the people in renewing the covenant. Moses dies on Mount Nebo, seeing the Promised Land from its summit.

Moses's successor, Joshua, sends spies into the land. In the fortified city of Jericho, Rahab, a prostitute, hides the spies in exchange for their promise of safety for her and her family when the Israelites attack.

Joshua leads the people across the Jordan River, which stops flowing long enough for them to cross. They march around Jericho with the ark of the covenant for seven days. On the seventh day, their priests sound shofars (rams' horns), the people shout, and Jericho's walls fall. Joshua orders Rahab and her family spared, but the rest of the city and all in it destroyed.

Achan keeps some treasure for himself, angering God. When they lose their next battle, at the small city of Ai, Achan confesses his disobedience. The Israelites stone and burn him, and God is no longer

Deuteronomy 17:1–Joshua 11:23

angry. When the Israelites attack Ai again, they defeat it. Their conquest of Canaan then continues.

Opening

- Begin with prayer.
- Invite a volunteer or volunteers to summarize the week's readings, using the overview above as a reference.
- Invite the group to share initial responses to the readings, as well as any questions they may have.
- Ask for volunteers to share some of their daily responses from this week from *The Bible Year* devotional.
- If you are using *The Bible Year* videos, play the video for today's session now.
- Continue your discussion of the week's Bible passages with the questions below.

Discussion Questions

1. How does Moses tell the Israelites they can recognize the prophet God will raise up for them in the future (Deuteronomy 18:15-22)? How can and do God's people recognize prophetic voices today?
2. Who, if anyone, do you consider a modern prophet, and why?
3. What does Moses command the people to do with their harvests' first fruits (26:1-11)? What purposes does this ritual serve, for the individual and the community? What rituals, if any, do you and your congregation observe that serve similar purposes?
4. Scholars suggest Moses's final song (32:1-43) reflects how Israel came to understand its defeat by foreign enemies centuries later. Why might a later editor place such a song in Moses's mouth? How can looking to the past help or hinder God's people as they seek to make sense of the present?

The Bible Year: Leader Guide

5. How is Rahab (Joshua 2) a model of faith for God's people today? Why is it significant that Matthew identifies her as an ancestor of Jesus (Matthew 1:5)?
6. What do the miracles in this week's chapters, from the halt of the Jordan's flow (Joshua 3:10-17) to Joshua's halting of the sun (10:12-14), signify about the Israelites' conquest of Canaan? How, if at all, are these miracles significant for you?
7. Archaeological findings don't generally support biblical stories about the conquest of Canaan. Why did Israel remember and retell its entrance into the land with these stories of violence and total destruction? What did these stories say to them about God, and what can they say to us about God today?

Closing

- Ask for several volunteers to summarize what they have found most meaningful about your discussion or about the biblical text this week. How might God be calling them to respond to it?
- Invite the group to raise any prayer concerns or lift up any reasons for joy and thanksgiving.
- Lead the group in a short closing prayer or invite a volunteer to do so.

38

SESSION 9

Joshua 12:1– Judges 16:31

Overview

The aged Joshua receives the promise that God will drive out the inhabitants of Canaan who are still unconquered and allots territories to the tribes of Israel. Joshua assembles the tribes at Shechem and recites their history with God, urging them to choose whom they will serve. The people pledge faithfulness to God and renew the covenant.

In the Book of Judges, after Joshua dies, because the Israelites have not driven all the Canaanites from the land, a cycle that will repeat itself for centuries to come begins:

- The Israelites worship the Canaanites' gods.
- God gives the Israelites over to their enemies.
- The Israelites cry out to God.
- God raises up a deliverer who saves the Israelites.
- After the judge's death, the Israelites again worship the Canaanites' gods.

The "judges" are more divinely empowered military leaders than legal authorities. They include:

- Deborah, who goes with Barak and his forces into battle against the Canaanite commander Sisera (who is killed by a non-Israelite woman, Jael).
- Gideon, who defeats the Midianites with only three hundred men, but who also later makes a golden idol.
- Jephthah, who defeats the Ammonites but whose rash vow to God leads him to sacrifice his daughter.
- Samson, who wins victories against the Philistines, his greatest being the destruction of their temple when he is their captive, dying among them in its ruins.

Opening

- Begin with prayer.
- Invite a volunteer or volunteers to summarize the week's readings, using the overview above as a reference.
- Invite the group to share initial responses to the readings, as well as any questions they may have.
- Ask for volunteers to share some of their daily responses from this week from *The Bible Year* devotional.
- If you are using *The Bible Year* videos, play the video for today's session now.
- Continue your discussion of the week's Bible passages with the questions below.

Discussion Questions

1. Why, when the Israelites at Shechem promise to serve God, does Joshua tell them they cannot (Joshua 24:19)? Who has challenged you and your congregation about how seriously you take your commitments to God, and how? How do their challenges continue to shape your faith?
2. Why does God decide against driving out the rest of the Canaanites (Judges 2:20-23; compare Joshua 13:6)? Why, despite this decision, does God continue

Joshua 12:1–Judges 16:31

to intervene by raising up judges to save the Israelites (Judges 2:15-19)? What historical realities does this framework explain? What claims about God does it make? How, if at all, does it matter for Christians today?

3. How would you describe Deborah and Jael (Judges 4–5)? Why does Barak refuse to go into battle without Deborah? Why does Jael, who is not an Israelite, kill Sisera? Do you think Jael's act is praiseworthy (5:24-27)? Why or why not?

4. Why and how does Gideon seek signs and assurances from God (6:11-24, 36-40)? How does God respond? Have you ever asked for signs and assurances from God? What happened?

5. The author of Hebrews remembers Gideon (chapters 6–8), Jephthah (chapter 11), and Samson (chapters 13–16) among the models of faith (Hebrews 11:32). Having read their stories, would you agree? Why or why not? What does Hebrews' inclusion of these three judges in the "great cloud of witnesses" (Hebrews 12:1) suggest about the people through whom God chooses to work?

6. With which, if any, of the Israelites' judges do you most identify, and why?

Closing

- Ask for several volunteers to summarize what they have found most meaningful about your discussion or about the biblical text this week. How might God be calling them to respond to it?
- Invite the group to raise any prayer concerns or lift up any reasons for joy and thanksgiving.
- Lead the group in a short closing prayer or invite a volunteer to do so.

SESSION 10

Judges 17:1– 1 Samuel 15:35

Overview

When men from the tribe of Benjamin rape and leave for dead a woman who is concubine to a Levite, the Levite cuts up her body and sends it to the tribes, inciting civil war. The Book of Judges ends on a note of horror.

Yet goodness isn't entirely absent during the judges' days, as the Book of Ruth illustrates. Ruth, a woman from Moab, accompanies her Israelite mother-in-law, Naomi, back to Bethlehem after Naomi's husband and sons die. Boaz, a landowner and kinsman to Naomi, makes special provisions for Ruth when he sees her gleaning in his fields. At Ruth's suggestion—made in ambiguous but suggestive circumstances—Boaz marries Ruth and buys back the land that belonged to Naomi's dead husband.

The Book of Samuel (written as one book) begins by telling of its title character's birth and childhood serving at the Israelites' central sanctuary in Shiloh. In time, Samuel becomes the last "judge" of Israel. When the Israelites demand a king, Samuel, following God's instructions, anoints Saul to rule. Saul enjoys early victories against Israel's foes, but impatiently offers a sacrifice to God without Samuel to maintain the Israelites' favor.

Judges 17:1–1 Samuel 15:35

He also spares the Amalekites' king and the best of their livestock despite God's order that the enemy and all they owned be totally destroyed. God is sorry for choosing Saul as king.

Opening

- Begin with prayer.
- Invite a volunteer or volunteers to summarize the week's readings, using the overview above as a reference.
- Invite the group to share initial responses to the readings, as well as any questions they may have.
- Ask for volunteers to share some of their daily responses from this week from *The Bible Year* devotional.
- If you are using *The Bible Year* videos, play the video for today's session now.
- Continue your discussion of the week's Bible passages with the questions below.

Discussion Questions

1. In the Judges's closing chapters, the narrator tells us "each person did what they thought to be right" (17:6; 21:25). How does this moral chaos show itself in these chapters? How much, if at all, do you think the narrator's assessment could describe moral conditions today?

2. What is the church's responsibility in a society where people disagree and generally have the right to do what they think is correct?

3. The central problem in the book named for Ruth is restoring or "redeeming" Naomi's life—her land, her status, her happiness. How does God act as "restorer of life" (4:15) through the various characters' actions? How does Ruth's place in King David's (4:22) and Jesus's genealogies (Matthew 1:5) reinforce the book's theme of redemption? What actions, even small ones, could you take to help restore someone's life today?

4. What does Samuel's birth represent for his mother Hannah (1 Samuel 1:1–2:10)? Why is she willing to dedicate the child she has wanted for so long to God's service at Shiloh? What lessons about faith and gratitude might Hannah teach us?
5. In 1 Samuel 8, why do the Israelites want a king? Why does Samuel warn them about their desire for one? Why do you think God grants their request?
6. What problems have you seen arise when God's people, collectively or individually, don't want to maintain their distinctive identity?
7. What are Saul's strengths as Israel's first king? What are his weaknesses? What do you think about God's decision to reject Saul as king?

Closing

- Ask for several volunteers to summarize what they have found most meaningful about your discussion or about the biblical text this week. How might God be calling them to respond to it?
- Invite the group to raise any prayer concerns or lift up any reasons for joy and thanksgiving.
- Lead the group in a short closing prayer or invite a volunteer to do so.

SESSION 11

1 Samuel 16:1–
2 Samuel 7:29

Overview

Samuel anoints David, son of Jesse, a shepherd boy from Bethlehem, to be Israel's next king. David enters Saul's service as a musician. He kills Goliath, the Philistines' giant champion, using only a stone in his slingshot and his trust in God.

David and Saul's son Jonathan make a covenant of loving friendship, and David marries Saul's daughter Michal; but Saul himself fears David will become king from the day David kills Goliath. After Saul hurls a spear at David as David plays the harp for him, Michal helps David escape, and Jonathan makes excuses for David's absence from court. But Saul is intent on hunting David down.

David faces wilderness adventure and hardship as he flees from Saul. Twice, he spares the king's life. Ultimately, Jonathan and his brothers die in battle with the Philistines, and Saul kills himself rather than let the Philistines kill him.

After a long civil war, the tribes of Israel unite to anoint David as their king. David makes Jerusalem his capital and brings the ark of the covenant to it in a festival procession. Though David wants to build a house (a temple) for God, the prophet Nathan tells him God has promised to build David a house (a dynasty) that will rule God's people forever.

Opening

- Begin with prayer.
- Invite a volunteer or volunteers to summarize the week's readings, using the overview above as a reference.
- Invite the group to share initial responses to the readings, as well as any questions they may have.
- Ask for volunteers to share some of their daily responses from this week from *The Bible Year* devotional.
- If you are using *The Bible Year* videos, play the video for today's session now.
- Continue your discussion of the week's Bible passages with the questions below.

Discussion Questions

1. What makes David a surprising choice for king (1 Samuel 16:6-12)? What signs, if any, do you find in this week's chapters that God has prepared David to be king?
2. When has someone surprised you because you judged them on their "outward appearance"?
3. The story of David and Goliath has become proverbial for any "underdog" going up against an overwhelming adversary, but David doesn't see himself as an underdog (17:32-37, 45-47). Why not? When have you felt like an underdog? How did you handle the situation? When, if ever, might an "underdog" have seen *you* as their "Goliath," and what happened?
4. Both Jonathan and Michal help David escape their father Saul because they love David (chapters 18–20). Have you ever helped someone despite opposition

from your family (however defined)? What happened? Would you do so again? Why or why not?
5. Why does David twice spare Saul's life (chapters 24, 26)? What do these incidents reveal about David's character and convictions?
6. When have you chosen mercy when you could have benefited from choosing differently? When has another person shown you unmerited mercy? How did you respond?
7. Why and how does Abigail act as a peacemaker in 1 Samuel 25? Have you ever appealed for peace on behalf of someone who would never do so themselves? What happened?
8. Relocating the ark of the covenant to Jerusalem is a political gesture as much as a pious one (2 Samuel 6). How do you see leaders today using religious speech and action for political ends? When, if ever, is it appropriate for people in power to do so?
9. How is God's promise of a dynasty to David an expression of God's grace (2 Samuel 7)? Why is this promise significant for Christians (Matthew 1:1; Luke 1:32-33)?

Closing

- Ask for several volunteers to summarize what they have found most meaningful about your discussion or about the biblical text this week. How might God be calling them to respond to it?
- Invite the group to raise any prayer concerns or lift up any reasons for joy and thanksgiving.
- Lead the group in a short closing prayer or invite a volunteer to do so.

SESSION 12

2 Samuel 8:1– 1 Kings 11:43

Overview

The bright promise with which King David's reign over a united Israel began is quickly overshadowed by his sin. In lust he takes Bathsheba, who is married to his faithful soldier, Uriah. David orders Uriah deliberately placed where the fighting is fiercest so he is killed, then takes Bathsheba as a wife. The prophet Nathan announces God's condemnation of David. David repents and Nathan conveys God's forgiveness. Despite God's forgiveness, David and Bathsheba's child dies.

David's son Amnon rapes his half-sister Tamar. When David fails to punish Amnon, David's son Absalom has Amnon killed. In time, Absalom mounts a rebellion against his father, and David and his court must flee Jerusalem. The rebellion ends when Absalom meets a bizarre, gruesome death.

More warfare mars David's last years, as well a census of Israel the king orders that angers God, who punishes the land with a plague.

In the Book of Kings (written as one book), Solomon—David and Bathsheba's second child—succeeds his father. He prays for wisdom as his reign begins, and God grants it, along with wealth and fame. Solomon also does what his father did not: He has a magnificent Temple to God built in Jerusalem. But like his father, Solomon strays from God's ways. To please his many non-Israelite wives, he builds altars to their foreign gods. God vows to take the kingdom from Solomon, and rebellion erupts even before the king dies.

Opening

- Begin with prayer.
- Invite a volunteer or volunteers to summarize the week's readings, using the overview above as a reference.
- Invite the group to share initial responses to the readings, as well as any questions they may have.
- Ask for volunteers to share some of their daily responses from this week from *The Bible Year* devotional.
- If you are using *The Bible Year* videos, play the video for today's session now.
- Continue your discussion of the week's Bible passages with the questions below.

Discussion Questions

1. Throughout this week's chapters, men in power abuse their power by violating women (David and Bathsheba; Amnon and Tamar; Absalom and his father's concubines). How does or how could your congregation help and support women who are victims of sexual abuse? What do or could you personally do?
2. Through Nathan, God tells David his family will never know peace because of his sin (2 Samuel 12:10-11). How does or how should the church today speak truth to power as Nathan did? Who are the voices acting as Nathan *to* the church, speaking truths we would rather not hear but need to hear in order to live faithfully?
3. When have you seen the lasting effects of sin across multiple generations? What does this say about the human condition and the need for God's grace?

The Bible Year: Leader Guide

Where do you see signs of God redeeming sin that is generations old?
4. David laments Absalom even though Absalom rebelled against him (18:19-33). How much, if at all, can you identify with David's grief? How does or how could your church support parents and children in broken relationships?
5. Reread King David's last words (23:1-7). Having read the stories of David's reign and family, how do you react to these words? Do they seem a fitting summation of David's life and legacy? Why or why not?
6. King Solomon's God-given wisdom is legendary (1 Kings 3; 10:1-5, 23-24). Who is the wisest person you have known? Why?
7. What was special about the Temple in Jerusalem (6:11-13)? How does Solomon's dedicatory prayer recognize both God's transcendence and God's nearness (8:27-30)? How does your congregation's worship recognize these two dimensions of God's relationship to us?

Closing

+ Ask for several volunteers to summarize what they have found most meaningful about your discussion or about the biblical text this week. How might God be calling them to respond to it?
+ Invite the group to raise any prayer concerns or lift up any reasons for joy and thanksgiving.
+ Lead the group in a short closing prayer or invite a volunteer to do so.

SESSION 13

1 Kings 12:1–
2 Kings 17:41

Overview

After Solomon's death, his son, Rehoboam, announces he will demand even more money and labor from the Israelites than his father did. Ten of the tribes make Jeroboam, who rebelled against Solomon, their king. The tribes of Judah and Benjamin recognize Rehoboam as king. For the next two centuries, God's people are divided: the Northern Kingdom, Israel, with Samaria as its capital; and the Southern Kingdom, Judah, with Jerusalem its capital.

The rest of Kings follows the reigns of Israel's and Judah's monarchs. The book judges whether each ruler sins. Most do, failing both God and their subjects. Jeroboam sets a pattern of idolatry in Israel that many later kings continue.

Kings also tells of two important prophets. Elijah challenges the worship of the Canaanite storm god Baal in Israel, an idolatry promoted by King Ahab and Queen Jezebel. His confrontation and massacre of Baal's prophets on Mount Carmel follows a dramatic display of God's power. After Elijah ascends to heaven in a whirlwind, his disciple Elisha continues declaring God's message.

More kings rise and fall. When King Hoshea of Israel refuses to pay tribute to the Assyrian Empire, Assyria invades and carries the Israelites away—divine judgment on the Northern Kingdom's idolatry, leaving the Southern Kingdom alone in the Promised Land.

Opening

- Begin with prayer.
- Invite a volunteer or volunteers to summarize the week's readings, using the overview above as a reference.
- Invite the group to share initial responses to the readings, as well as any questions they may have.
- Ask for volunteers to share some of their daily responses from this week from *The Bible Year* devotional.
- If you are using *The Bible Year* videos, play the video for today's session now.
- Continue your discussion of the week's Bible passages with the questions below.

Discussion Questions

1. What causes Israel's division (1 Kings 12:1-24)? What does Rehoboam's choice of whose advice to take (12:8) suggest about the promise and peril of generational changes in a society?
2. How do older and younger generations in your congregation work together to discern and do God's will?
3. What are your impressions of Elijah (1 Kings 17–21; 2 Kings 1-2)? What do you admire about him? What do you not admire?
4. What do you think Elijah hopes to gain by fleeing to Mount Horeb (Sinai) in 1 Kings 19? What do you make of God's response (19:9-18)? What do you do when God isn't present to you in ways you expect or hope?

5. How and why do Ahab and Jezebel get Naboth's vineyard (1 Kings 21)? What does this story tell us about God's expectations for people in power? What is our responsibility when we see those in authority abusing power?
6. One of Elisha's most famous miracles is the healing of Naaman, who commands the army of Israel's enemy Aram (2 Kings 5). Why does Elisha offer a way to health to Naaman? Why does Naaman initially resist it?
7. Why is Gehazi punished with Naaman's skin disease? What does this story show us about serving God?
8. How do you react to Kings' explanation of why Assyria conquered Israel (2 Kings 17:7-18)? Given the book focuses on how Israel's kings didn't abandon "the way of Jeroboam," is it just to judge the whole nation as idolatrous (consider also 1 Kings 19:18)?
9. To what extent do you judge your society by the virtues or failings of its leaders? How do you think God works through nations' triumphs and defeats today?

Closing

- Ask for several volunteers to summarize what they have found most meaningful about your discussion or about the biblical text this week. How might God be calling them to respond to it?
- Invite the group to raise any prayer concerns or lift up any reasons for joy and thanksgiving.
- Lead the group in a short closing prayer or invite a volunteer to do so.

SESSION 14

2 Kings 18:1–
1 Chronicles 27:34

Overview

King Hezekiah of Judah is one of the few monarchs the Book of Kings praises. He dismantles idolatrous worship. He stays faithful when Sennacherib of Assyria besieges Jerusalem. God even adds fifteen years to Hezekiah's life after an illness. But through the prophet Isaiah, God judges Hezekiah for showing his treasures to messengers from Babylon, and tells him the Babylonian Empire will plunder Judah in the future.

King Manasseh, Hezekiah's son, rules in contrast to his father, reintroducing the worship of foreign gods and killing innocents. God decrees disaster for Judah as a result.

Decades later, King Josiah is a righteous ruler. When the high priest discovers "the book of the law" (likely much of what we know as Deuteronomy) in the Temple and the prophet Huldah confirms its authenticity, Josiah reforms Judah's worship in line with its precepts.

But God does not change the divine decision. After Josiah dies, Nebuchadnezzar of Babylon besieges Jerusalem, and King Jehoiachin surrenders himself and his court to him. Nebuchadnezzar takes the king's and the Temple's treasures. Eleven years later, he again attacks, destroys the Temple, and takes most of the rest of Judah's population into exile.

2 Kings 18:1–1 Chronicles 27:34

The Book of Chronicles (written as one book) recounts Israel's history beginning with King Saul's death. The chronicler highlights David's military victories, his ordering of Israel's worship, and his preparing Solomon to build the Temple.

Opening

- Begin with prayer.
- Invite a volunteer or volunteers to summarize the week's readings, using the overview above as a reference.
- Invite the group to share initial responses to the readings, as well as any questions they may have.
- Ask for volunteers to share some of their daily responses from this week from *The Bible Year* devotional.
- If you are using *The Bible Year* videos, play the video for today's session now.
- Continue your discussion of the week's Bible passages with the questions below.

Discussion Questions

1. How does Hezekiah respond when the Assyrians tell him and his subjects to abandon their trust in God (2 Kings 18–19)? When has your congregation or when have you personally felt "under siege"? Were you able to take your worries and fears to God, as Hezekiah did (19:14-19)? If so, how? If not, why not?
2. Who has ever been to you as Isaiah was to Hezekiah, encouraging you to remain steadfast in faith, and how?
3. When he reacts to Isaiah's prophecy regarding Babylon and Judah (20:12-19), is Hezekiah displaying acceptance or fatalism? How so? About what issues does your congregation need to be looking beyond your own days?
4. What about you and your family? How does faith in God encourage us to act for the well-being of future generations?

5. Why do Manasseh's sins (21:1-16) mark a kind of "red line" or "last straw" for God? Do you believe God has a "breaking point" with the immorality of nations, churches, and/or individuals? Why or why not?
6. Who is Huldah, and what is her message from God for Josiah (22:14-20)? Have you or has your congregation ever received a message of judgment mixed with mercy? from whom? How did you respond?
7. Kings ends by drawing attention to Jehoiachin's fate in Babylon (25:27-30). Do you find this a hopeful ending to the book? Why or why not?
8. The chronicler presents a far more favorable view of David than Kings does. Why doesn't the book include the stories of David's moral failings and family strife? How does the Bible's double rehearsal of David's reign affect your understanding of him and his significance?

Closing

+ Ask for several volunteers to summarize what they have found most meaningful about your discussion or about the biblical text this week. How might God be calling them to respond to it?
+ Invite the group to raise any prayer concerns or lift up any reasons for joy and thanksgiving.
+ Lead the group in a short closing prayer or invite a volunteer to do so.

SESSION 15

1 Chronicles 28:1– 2 Chronicles 24:27

Overview

After David's death, Solomon organizes the building of the Temple in Jerusalem. God appears to Solomon and, in addition to warning about the Temple's destruction should the people break the covenant, promises to forgive them when they humbly repent.

Civil war splits the kingdom. The chronicler mainly focuses on the reigns of Judah's rulers. When King Rehoboam leads the nation away from God's law, Shishak of Egypt attacks and captures the king's and Temple's treasures. God spares the king and his court when they repent.

King Abijah wins a military victory against Israel. His son Asa dismantles idolatrous worship, and God defeats an invasion from Ethiopia for him; however, when Asa later trusts his alliance with Aram against Israel, God promises Judah's wars will continue.

Facing invasion from enemies, Asa's son Jehoshaphat leads the nation in prayer. God responds by causing the invaders to destroy each other. Yet Jehoshaphat also provokes God's anger by allying on occasion with Israel.

Violence and apostasy mark the reigns of Jehoshaphat's successors. Athaliah, Ahab and Jezebel's daughter, even usurps Judah's throne and desecrates the Temple. The priest Jehoiada leads an armed revolt to restore David's line to power. But after Jehoiada's death, King Joash leads Judah back into idolatry.

Opening

- Begin with prayer.
- Invite a volunteer or volunteers to summarize the week's readings, using the overview above as a reference.
- Invite the group to share initial responses to the readings, as well as any questions they may have.
- Ask for volunteers to share some of their daily responses from this week from *The Bible Year* devotional.
- If you are using *The Bible Year* videos, play the video for today's session now.
- Continue your discussion of the week's Bible passages with the questions below.

Discussion Questions

1. God's promise to hear the people's prayers of humble repentance directed toward the Temple (2 Chronicles 7:12-15) is unique to Chronicles' account of God's second appearance to Solomon (compare 1 Kings 9:1-9). Where did you notice people repenting in this week's chapters? If Chronicles was, as many scholars think, written for the Jews who returned to the land after the Babylonian Exile, why might the theme of repentance matter to them?
2. How important is repentance in your own faith, and in the life of your congregation?
3. How do 1 Kings 15:1-8 and 2 Chronicles 13 present Abijam/Abijah differently? What do you think accounts for these differences? What do they suggest about why the Bible contains these two accounts of Israel and Judah's history?

4. Kings includes relatively little about Jehoshaphat (1 Kings 15:24; 22:1-50), but 2 Chronicles 17–21 details his reign. What is your impression of him? How does his prayer in 2 Chronicles 20 and God's response illustrate the promise God made to Solomon in 2 Chronicles 7? What lessons about faith might you and your congregation learn from Jehoshaphat?
5. How does Athaliah threaten the dynasty promised to David and Solomon (1 Kings 11; 2 Chronicles 22:10–23:21)? How do Jehoshabeath and Jehoiada preserve the royal line? What do these events suggest about the security of God's promises? What do you imagine Chronicles' first audience thought about them? What do you and your congregation think about them?
6. Once Jehoiada dies, King Joash, whom Jehoiada set on the throne, yields to other influences who lead him—and through him, the nation—astray (2 Chronicles 24:15-22). Where have we seen this dynamic at work before in Israel and Judah's history? How can God's people help a society remain faithful to God as generations pass?

Closing

+ Ask for several volunteers to summarize what they have found most meaningful about your discussion or about the biblical text this week. How might God be calling them to respond to it?
+ Invite the group to raise any prayer concerns or lift up any reasons for joy and thanksgiving.
+ Lead the group in a short closing prayer or invite a volunteer to do so.

SESSION 16

2 Chronicles 25:1–Nehemiah 4:23

Overview

Judah's next several kings reign in accordance with God's will—mostly. The chronicler relates ways they depart from total obedience to God. Kings Hezekiah and Josiah are the exceptions, whom the chronicler praises for following God faithfully.

Jerusalem ultimately falls to Babylon, but Chronicles ends with King Cyrus of Persia (who defeated the Babylonian Empire in 539 BCE) calling on the exiles from Judah to return home and rebuild God's Temple.

The Book of Ezra begins at this historical point. Exiles do go back and begin rebuilding, but opposition from non-Jews in the land delays the work until Cyrus's successor, Darius, intervenes.

Fifty-eight years after the Temple's dedication, Ezra himself arrives from Babylon, a priest and scribe sent from Persia's King Artaxerxes to help restore Judah's worship and legal systems. When Ezra arrives and finds the people have married non-Jews, Ezra initiates a months-long investigation and dissolution of mixed marriages, and the Jewish men send their non-Jewish wives and children away.

2 Chronicles 25:1–Nehemiah 4:23

King Artaxerxes also sends to his cupbearer Nehemiah to Judah to help the community recover. Nehemiah spearheads the project of rebuilding the walls of Jerusalem, as well as a military effort to protect the work from foreign enemies.

Opening

- Begin with prayer.
- Invite a volunteer or volunteers to summarize the week's readings, using the overview above as a reference.
- Invite the group to share initial responses to the readings, as well as any questions they may have.
- Ask for volunteers to share some of their daily responses from this week from *The Bible Year* devotional.
- If you are using *The Bible Year* videos, play the video for today's session now.
- Continue your discussion of the week's Bible passages with the questions below.

Discussion Questions

1. How does Hezekiah attempt to unify God's divided people (2 Chronicles 30)? How would you evaluate his success? When and how have you seen worship unite a divided community?
2. The Book of Kings depicts Hezekiah's son Manasseh as an unambiguously bad ruler (2 Kings 21:1-20). How does the chronicler cast him a slightly different light (2 Chronicles 33:10-17)? Why do you think the chronicler does this?
3. What hope might the community who returned to the land after exile in Babylon have found in Manasseh's story? What hope might his story hold for you and your congregation?
4. Much of the literature in the Old Testament tries to make sense out of Babylon's conquest of Judah. How

does the explanation in Second Chronicles of why this disaster happened (36:11-21) compare with the explanation given in 2 Kings 21:10-15? How do these explanations contradict or complement each other? What does the chronicler want to communicate by ending the book with Cyrus's decree?
5. How and why does the Book of Ezra stress the importance of maintaining clear distinctions between who does and does not belong to God's people (Ezra 4; 9–10)? When, if ever, do God's people need to make these distinctions clear today?
6. When, if ever, might we need to rethink the limits of our communities? How has welcoming those once regarded as foreigners or outsiders into your congregation enriched its worship and work?
7. The people's enemies taunt and threaten Nehemiah and his wall-builders for their work (Nehemiah 4). When, if ever, has your congregation encountered opposition for obeying God's will? How did you respond? What happened?
8. Should God's people today pray against their enemies as Nehemiah did (4:4-5)? Why or why not?

Closing

- Ask for several volunteers to summarize what they have found most meaningful about your discussion or about the biblical text this week. How might God be calling them to respond to it?
- Invite the group to raise any prayer concerns or lift up any reasons for joy and thanksgiving.
- Lead the group in a short closing prayer or invite a volunteer to do so.

SESSION 17

Nehemiah 5:1– Job 14:22

Overview

After Jerusalem's walls are rebuilt, the people gather to hear Ezra read God's law aloud. The reading leads the people to more faithful obedience: observing the festivals in the law, separating themselves from non-Israelites (including wives of foreign ancestry), and confessing their nation's sins. Nehemiah, the priests and Levites, and the people's leaders sign a solemn pledge to obey God's law.

The Book of Esther relates how Esther, a young Jewish woman, is chosen by the Persian king Ahasuerus to be his new queen. Esther's uncle Mordecai learns Haman, one of the king's favored officials, plots the destruction of the Jewish people. At Mordecai's urging, Esther reveals herself as a Jew to Ahasuerus and exposes Haman's plot against her people. Haman is hanged upon the same gallows he had built to hang Mordecai.

The title character in the Book of Job is a righteous man, blameless before God and esteemed by his society. But when Satan accuses Job of loving God only because God has materially blessed him, God puts Job and all he has in Satan's power. In rapid succession, Job loses his property, children, and health. Job refuses to curse God but does bitterly lament his suffering. Three of his friends offer various explanations for Job's suffering, but Job rejects them all, desiring to make his case directly to God.

Opening

- Begin with prayer.
- Invite a volunteer or volunteers to summarize the week's readings, using the overview above as a reference.
- Invite the group to share initial responses to the readings, as well as any questions they may have.
- Ask for volunteers to share some of their daily responses from this week from *The Bible Year* devotional.
- If you are using *The Bible Year* videos, play the video for today's session now.
- Continue your discussion of the week's Bible passages with the questions below.

Discussion Questions

1. Why do the people weep when they hear God's law read to them? Why are they told not to weep (Nehemiah 8:9-11)? What is the difference between weeping and confession (Nehemiah 9) and recommitment to God (Nehemiah 10)?
2. Has hearing or reading Scripture ever moved you to confession and recommitment? If so, how did you respond?
3. What corporate practices of confession and recommitment does your congregation observe? How have they made a difference in your congregation's life?
4. God is never named in Esther. How do you think God is present in this story? What does Esther's story suggest about how God may be at work in your life and your congregation's life?

5. What motivates Haman's hatred for Mordecai and "all the Jews" in Persia (Esther 3:5-6)? Where do you see anti-Jewish hatred in society today? How much historical responsibility do Christians bear for anti-Judaism? How does your congregation reject anti-Jewish hate and support your Jewish neighbors?
6. Mordecai tells Esther she may have risen to royal status "for a moment like this" (4:14) or as some translations have it: "for just a time as this." How do we know whether we are in such a time for using the influence and authority we have for good, despite risks to ourselves?
7. The reversals in Esther include not only Haman dying on the gallows he prepared for Mordecai but also Jews throughout the Persian Empire killing their enemies with the king's approval (9:1-17). When in history have oppressed peoples become oppressors? How has the church, in its history, turned from persecuted to persecutor? What can God's people today do to break this violent cycle?
8. Do you think God and Satan's arrangements concerning Job (in Job 1 and 2) accurately represent how God deals with human beings? Why or why not?

Closing

- Ask for several volunteers to summarize what they have found most meaningful about your discussion or about the biblical text this week. How might God be calling them to respond to it?
- Invite the group to raise any prayer concerns or lift up any reasons for joy and thanksgiving.
- Lead the group in a short closing prayer or invite a volunteer to do so.

SESSION 18

Job 15:1–
Psalm 12:8

Overview

Against all his friends' suggestions that he somehow deserves his suffering, Job asserts his innocence and integrity. God gets the last word in the discussion. God answers Job out of a whirlwind—confronting him with creation's vast size and immense diversity, challenging him to display the power God wields. A humbled but apparently satisfied Job receives more children and material prosperity than he previously had, and lives to a ripe old age.

The Psalms are the songs ancient Israel used to worship God—formally and informally, as assemblies and as individuals. The Psalter attributes about half of its 150 psalms to King David.

The first dozen psalms give some idea of the Psalter's range of tone and topics. They include psalms praising God's wisdom and justice; psalms about God's relationship to the king enthroned on Mount Zion in Jerusalem, as well as to other nations; prayers for deliverance from illness and enemies; and songs of confident trust in God. Diverse as they are, the psalms all contain believers' honest and heartfelt communication with God.

Job 15:1–Psalm 12:8

Opening

- Begin with prayer.
- Invite a volunteer or volunteers to summarize the week's readings, using the overview above as a reference.
- Invite the group to share initial responses to the readings, as well as any questions they may have.
- Ask for volunteers to share some of their daily responses from this week from *The Bible Year* devotional.
- If you are using *The Bible Year* videos, play the video for today's session now.
- Continue your discussion of the week's Bible passages with the questions below.

Discussion Questions

1. "The patience of Job" is a proverbial expression. Based on his speeches in the book, would you describe Job as patient? Why or why not?
2. How do you react to Job's friends' attempts throughout the book to explain his suffering and defend God's ways? Why does Job respond to them as he does? When, if ever, have you heard similar "explanations" for your own suffering? When, if ever, have you offered similar "explanations" for others' suffering?
3. What is the best advice you have, as a person of faith, for helping someone who is suffering?
4. What is your opinion of God's response to Job (Job 38–41)? Does it offer satisfying answers to the issues Job has raised? Why or why not? What does Job seem to find satisfying about it (42:1-6)?
5. Why does God say Job's friends haven't spoken of correctly but that Job has (42:7-9)? What does God's "verdict" on the speeches of Job and his friends suggest about the place of lamentation and protest in a faithful relationship with God?

6. The Book of Job explores the age-old, vexing question of why bad things happen to good people. How does it help or hinder your thinking about this question?
7. What claims does Psalm 1 make about the ways of the wicked and of the righteous? How do you react to these claims, coming as they do immediately after the Book of Job?
8. Psalm 2 identifies the king as God's "anointed one" (in Hebrew, "messiah," v. 2) and God's "son" (v. 7). What did this psalm mean for ancient Israel? Why did it become an especially important psalm for Christians? How can people of faith understand its claims about the king's rule today?
9. What does Psalm 8 tell us about humanity's place in God's creation? What is your congregation doing and what are you doing personally to "rule over your handiwork"(v. 6) (to exercise "dominion" in NRSV) over the world in ways that nourish rather than threaten the natural world?

Closing

- Ask for several volunteers to summarize what they have found most meaningful about your discussion or about the biblical text this week. How might God be calling them to respond to it?
- Invite the group to raise any prayer concerns or lift up any reasons for joy and thanksgiving.
- Lead the group in a short closing prayer or invite a volunteer to do so.

SESSION 19

Psalms 13:1–41:13

Overview

Composed by many people over many centuries, the Psalter as we have it is divided into five books, possibly to mirror the five books of the Torah (Genesis to Deuteronomy). This week's psalms bring us to the end of Book I.

Our readings this week begin with Psalm 13, an individual's plaintive call for God's help. The psalm-singer—identified in the superscription, or heading, as David—doesn't hesitate to demand God save him from death. But as do most psalms of lament, Psalm 13 ends in praise, as though the very act of calling to God leads to renewed confidence in God's power.

Psalm 22, another lamentation, reflects the same dynamic, moving from deep despair to an exuberant hope that encompasses the whole earth. Psalm 23, a deeply personal depiction of God as a guiding and protecting shepherd, exudes a wholehearted trust in God.

Several psalms stress the morality of holiness God expects of God's people (for example, Psalms 15, 24). Other psalms acknowledge God's people fall short of these standards, but can confess, repent, and receive God's forgiveness when they do (for instance, Psalms 32, 39).

Opening

+ Begin with prayer.

The Bible Year: Leader Guide

- Invite a volunteer or volunteers to summarize the week's readings, using the overview above as a reference.
- Invite the group to share initial responses to the readings, as well as any questions they may have.
- Ask for volunteers to share some of their daily responses from this week from *The Bible Year* devotional.
- If you are using *The Bible Year* videos, play the video for today's session now.
- Continue your discussion of the week's Bible passages with the questions below.

Discussion Questions

1. What words, phrases, and images from this week's psalms most attracted your attention? Which ones surprised or challenged you the most? If you were to choose a favorite verse from this week's psalms, what would it be, and why?
2. What, if anything, has ever driven you to lament to God as the psalm-singers often do? What in the world, your community, or your life is worth lamenting to God?
3. How much does your congregation use the language of lament in its worship? Why do you think the Psalter contains so many examples of lamentation?
4. Psalm 19 says the heavens declare God's glory (vv. 1-6), and also praises God for God's commandments (vv. 7-13). How does God's instruction help you recognize and respond to God in the natural world?
5. Christians sometimes find it difficult to read Psalm 22 as about anyone *but* Jesus, yet God's people found and continue to find it meaningful apart from his story. How does this psalm speak, or how can you imagine it speaking, to someone who feels forsaken by God today?
6. Psalm 23 is easily the most famous and beloved psalm in the Bible, even though its shepherd imagery is foreign

to many modern people's daily experience. What other images for God can you think of that might convey the psalm's meaning to readers in your society today?
7. What connections does Psalm 32 suggest between sin, confession, and well-being? How have you experienced confession's power to heal in your own life? In the life of your congregation or wider community?

Closing

- Ask for several volunteers to summarize what they have found most meaningful about your discussion or about the biblical text this week. How might God be calling them to respond to it?
- Invite the group to raise any prayer concerns or lift up any reasons for joy and thanksgiving.
- Lead the group in a short closing prayer or invite a volunteer to do so.

SESSION 20

Psalms 42:1–68:35

Overview

Book II of the Psalter begins with both individual and national lament. The single psalm-singer voices an intense longing to be in God's presence and for delivery from foes (Psalms 42–43), while the community grapples with the gap between God's past deeds and their present suffering (Psalm 44).

But many of this week's psalms celebrate God's presence with and defense of God's people. Psalm 48, for instance, illustrates the central role Mount Zion played in ancient Israel's faith. Because Zion was the site of the Jerusalem Temple, where God's presence dwelled, some Israelites believed it impervious to attack, reflecting God's sovereignty over the nations. This belief made Babylon's defeat of Judah both a military-political and a spiritual crisis.

Several of this week's psalms (51, 52, 57, 63) are connected with events in King David's life. In particular, Psalm 51, attributed to David after his sin with and against Bathsheba, has served God's people as a paradigm of penance, giving us language to both confess our sin and trust in God's mercy.

This week's psalms end with a crescendo of calls for Israel and the world to thank and praise God for God's generous abundance and power to save.

Opening

- Begin with prayer.
- Invite a volunteer or volunteers to summarize the week's readings, using the overview above as a reference.
- Invite the group to share initial responses to the readings, as well as any questions they may have.
- Ask for volunteers to share some of their daily responses from this week from *The Bible Year* devotional.
- If you are using *The Bible Year* videos, play the video for today's session now.
- Continue your discussion of the week's Bible passages with the questions below.

Discussion Questions

1. What words, phrases, and images from this week's psalms most attracted your attention? Which ones surprised or challenged you the most? If you were to choose a favorite verse from this week's psalms, what would it be, and why?
2. Psalms 42 and 63 both sing of souls thirsting for God, and of the way worship with God's people can help quench that thirst. What kind of worship best satisfies your thirst for God, and why?
3. Psalm 46 assures the faithful that God is a "refuge and strength" (v. 1) amid natural disaster and warfare. When have you and your congregation most needed to hear this promise? When and how have you communicated this promise to your wider community?
4. Psalm 49 is a wisdom psalm, teaching about the way God has ordered human life. What lessons does the psalm-singer teach about wealth, death, and the connections between them?

The Bible Year: Leader Guide

5. Do you feel "overly impressed when someone becomes rich" (Psalm 49:16)? Why or why not? How might people of different economic standing hear and respond to this psalm differently?
6. Why does God testify against Israel in Psalm 50? What are the obligations of God's covenant people? What does this psalm tell us about the relationship between what we do in worship and what we do outside it?
7. Christian tradition counts Psalm 51 as one of seven "penitential psalms" (the others are Psalms 6, 32, 38, 102, 130, and 143).[1] How important are disciplines of confession and penance in your congregation's life? In your own life?
8. In Psalm 55, David prays about a friend's betrayal, even asking God to kill the former friend (vv. 15, 23). How, if at all, is this psalm a model for us as we pray when people we trust betray or otherwise fail us?

Closing

+ Ask for several volunteers to summarize what they have found most meaningful about your discussion or about the biblical text this week. How might God be calling them to respond to it?
+ Invite the group to raise any prayer concerns or lift up any reasons for joy and thanksgiving.
+ Lead the group in a short closing prayer or invite a volunteer to do so.

SESSION 21

Psalms 69:1–101:8

Overview

This week's psalms bring us almost to the end of Book IV. As in previous weeks, these psalms show God's people, individually and together, bringing a wide range of thoughts and feelings to God in prayer.

Psalm 72 is one of nine "royal psalms" focused on the role of Israel's monarch (the others being Psalms 2, 18, 20, 21, 45, 89, 110, and 132)[2] and one of only two attributed to Solomon (the other is Psalm 127). Psalm 72 offers a "job description" of an ideal king.

In Psalm 74, the singers express horror at Babylon's destruction of the Temple in Jerusalem (see also Psalm 79), yet express faith that God is still at work to save, despite their current distress.

Psalm 82 presents God in a council of other heavenly beings (see also Psalm 89:5-8), asserting God's sovereignty over them and demanding justice from all nations.

Psalm 88 is the only psalm of lament to end without any expression of hope.

Paraphrased in the Christmas carol "Joy to the World," Psalm 98 calls for celebration of God's imminent, righteous judgment of the earth.

Opening

+ Begin with prayer.

The Bible Year: Leader Guide

- Invite a volunteer or volunteers to summarize the week's readings, using the overview above as a reference.
- Invite the group to share initial responses to the readings, as well as any questions they may have.
- Ask for volunteers to share some of their daily responses from this week from *The Bible Year* devotional.
- If you are using *The Bible Year* videos, play the video for today's session now.
- Continue your discussion of the week's Bible passages with the questions below.

Discussion Questions

1. What words, phrases, and images from this week's psalms most attracted your attention? Which ones surprised or challenged you the most? If you were to choose a favorite verse from this week's psalms, what would it be, and why?
2. In Psalm 69, deep waters represent trouble and danger (compare Psalm 130). When was a time you would say you were sinking in the depths? What did you do? How did you escape the deep—or do you still feel "the waters have reached [your] neck" (v. 1)?
3. How do you and your congregation show God's "faithful love" (Psalm 69:16) to those in the depths?
4. How might Psalm 72 shape the way God's people pray for those in power over them, even when their leaders aren't kings? What does the psalm reveal about God's priorities and standards for those who exercise authority? What guidance does it offer God's people as we engage with social and political issues in our day?
5. In Psalm 77, how does the psalm-singer counter feelings of sorrow about God's apparent absence? When, if ever, has remembering the history of God with God's people helped you in times of spiritual distress?

6. As noted above, Psalm 88 is the only lament psalm in the Psalter that doesn't end in hope. Why do you think the Psalter includes it? What value do you see in its words and emotions?
7. How can Psalm 90 be a resource for God's people as we think about the reality of death? What are the "work of our hands" you want God to "last" (v. 17), and why?
8. What does integrity look like in Psalm 101? How confidently could—or should—you and your congregation claim this psalm today?
9. What should God's people do when they find failures of integrity in each other or in themselves?

Closing

- Ask for several volunteers to summarize what they have found most meaningful about your discussion or about the biblical text this week. How might God be calling them to respond to it?
- Invite the group to raise any prayer concerns or lift up any reasons for joy and thanksgiving.
- Lead the group in a short closing prayer or invite a volunteer to do so.

SESSION 22

Psalms 102:1–126:6

Overview

With this week's psalms we move from Book IV of the Psalter into Book V.

Psalms 105 and 106 recount much of Israel's history with God. Psalm 105 emphasizes God's gracious and mighty acts on Israel's behalf, especially in the exodus from Egypt (vv. 23-45). Psalm 106 emphasizes the people's sins, especially during their wilderness wanderings (vv. 13-33).

Psalm 107 spotlights four groups of people—desert wanderers (vv. 4-9), prisoners (vv. 10-16), sick sinners (vv. 17-22), and sailors (vv. 23-32)—who all call on God for help in distress, and receive it. They witness to God's "faithful love" (v. 1), a divine attribute the psalms frequently praise.

Psalm 110 is another royal psalm. Suitable for a king's coronation, it took on importance as a prophecy of a messiah for some later readers, including the early Christian church.

Psalm 117 is the shortest psalm, and Psalm 119 is the longest: a twenty-two-stanza poem (one for each Hebrew letter) extolling God's law as the source of light and life.

Psalms 120–126 begin a series of "songs of ascents," which pilgrims would sing as they walked up toward Jerusalem and Mount Zion to celebrate God's festivals.

Psalms 102:1–126:6

Opening

- Begin with prayer.
- Invite a volunteer or volunteers to summarize the week's readings, using the overview above as a reference.
- Invite the group to share initial responses to the readings, as well as any questions they may have.
- Ask for volunteers to share some of their daily responses from this week from *The Bible Year* devotional.
- If you are using *The Bible Year* videos, play the video for today's session now.
- Continue your discussion of the week's Bible passages with the questions below.

Discussion Questions

1. What words, phrases, and images from this week's psalms most attracted your attention? Which ones surprised or challenged you the most? If you were to choose a favorite verse from this week's psalms, what would it be, and why?

2. How does Psalm 104 draw attention to God's work in the natural world? How can it help us appreciate what we have in common with the rest of God's creatures? How should these connections shape the way we live with nature?

3. As noted, Psalms 105 and 106 offer two different perspectives on Israel's past, but what do these psalms have in common? How can this pair of psalms help your congregation and the wider church faithfully remember and retell their history with God?

4. In Psalm 107, God saves people who cry out in distress (vv. 6, 13, 19, 28). Were the psalm-singer composing this song today, what other groups of people in trouble might be included? What does wisely considering God's "faithful love" (v. 43) lead us to do for them?

5. What attributes and benefits of God's law most caught your attention as you read Psalm 119? Why? How like or unlike your own attitude toward studying Scripture is the psalm-singer's attitude toward studying God's law?
6. What practical things can we do to increase our desire to know and meditate on God's law?
7. Psalm 120, the first "song of ascents," sounds from a low place. What is the psalm-singer's situation? Have you ever found yourself in similar circumstances? What, if anything, did you do to rise above it? How does God help those surrounded by enemies of peace today?
8. How would the songs of ascents have encouraged travelers on their way to worship in Jerusalem? How does God use music to encourage God's people today? Does God speak to you through music? If so, how?

Closing

- Ask for several volunteers to summarize what they have found most meaningful about your discussion or about the biblical text this week. How might God be calling them to respond to it?
- Invite the group to raise any prayer concerns or lift up any reasons for joy and thanksgiving.
- Lead the group in a short closing prayer or invite a volunteer to do so.

SESSION 23

Psalm 127:1— Proverbs 3:35

Overview

The remaining psalms reflect the Psalter's range of emotion, from lamentation (for example, Psalm 137) and desperate pleas for help (Psalm 130) to thankful declarations of God's love (Psalm 136) and, especially at the Psalter's end, exuberant calls to praise God (Psalms 145–150).

The Book of Proverbs is one of the Bible's three great "Wisdom books." We have already read the first, Job, which largely questions much of the wisdom set forth in Proverbs (as will the Wisdom book following it, Ecclesiastes). The sages of ancient Israel whose teachings Proverbs preserves believed God embedded a moral order into the world at its creation. Proverbs defines wisdom and folly as righteous and unrighteous living and offers evidence of how God rewards the one and punishes the other. It is a didactic book in which fathers and other elders strive to shape young men's characters by teaching them how to align themselves with God's wisdom.

Proverbs often personifies wisdom as a woman, calling for humanity to heed her and live, warning those who ignore her of calamity to come. In contrast, those who find wisdom can expect health, security, abundance, and peace. The way to wisdom begins with honoring and trusting God.

Opening

- Begin with prayer.
- Invite a volunteer or volunteers to summarize the week's readings, using the overview above as a reference.
- Invite the group to share initial responses to the readings, as well as any questions they may have.
- Ask for volunteers to share some of their daily responses from this week from *The Bible Year* devotional.
- If you are using *The Bible Year* videos, play the video for today's session now.
- Continue your discussion of the week's Bible passages with the questions below.

Discussion Questions

1. Psalm 127 is the second of two psalms attributed to Solomon (the other is Psalm 72). How would this psalm be relevant to him? Are there any "construction projects" in your life you need to turn over to God? How will you do so?
2. Do you recognize your congregation in Psalm 133? Why or why not? How is unity different from uniformity? How can and do Christians work for unity among themselves? How can Christians act faithfully when they cannot achieve unity?
3. As a group, write your own call-and-response psalm modeled on Psalm 136. What events in your congregation's past and present point to God's faithful love?
4. If you were to write a version of Psalm 136 about your own life, what events would it include, and why?
5. Psalm 137 lays bare the pain and anger the Babylonian Exile caused, especially in verses 8-9. Have you ever

prayed with such anger? When? What happened? How do you think God responds to such prayers?
6. What difference does God's intimate knowledge of you and God's all-surrounding presence make to you day by day (Psalm 139)?
7. When have you felt most aware of God's nearness, and how did it make you feel? When, if ever, have you wanted to escape God's nearness, and why?
8. What is the relationship between God and wisdom (Proverbs 1:7; 2:6-8; 3:5-6, 19-20)? What are some of wisdom's benefits (3:13-18, 21-26)? What are the consequences of ignoring wisdom (1:20-33)? How have you experienced these benefits or consequences in your own life? in your congregation's life?

Closing

+ Ask for several volunteers to summarize what they have found most meaningful about your discussion or about the biblical text this week. How might God be calling them to respond to it?
+ Invite the group to raise any prayer concerns or lift up any reasons for joy and thanksgiving.
+ Lead the group in a short closing prayer or invite a volunteer to do so.

SESSION 24

Proverbs 4:1–15:33

Overview

In Proverbs 4–9, the sages continue exhorting youth to choose the way of wisdom and shun the way of folly. Fathers especially warn their sons against committing adultery—both the literal sin and the metaphorical lusting after ways that lead to ruin. The sages personify both wisdom and foolishness as women, each issuing invitations and making promises to mortals. Woman Wisdom promises honor, riches, and God's favor. Woman Folly promises pleasure, but delivers only death.

Proverbs 10 begins a long section (running through 22:16) of sayings attributed to King Solomon. The proverbs offer practical, ethical instruction on such topics as:

- The correlation between diligence and prosperity (examples: 10:4; 11:24; 14:23).
- The importance of speaking honestly and prudently (examples: 10:11; 12:17; 13:3).
- The necessity of honest labor and honest dealings in commerce (examples: 10:2; 11:1; 12:14).
- The value of kindness and generosity (examples: 11:17; 14:21; 15:1).

- The transitory nature of wealth and appearances (examples: 11:4, 22; 15:16).
- The necessity of disciplining children (examples: 13:1, 24; 15:5).
- The importance of obeying God's commands (examples: 14:2, 9; 15:33).

Opening

- Begin with prayer.
- Invite a volunteer or volunteers to summarize the week's readings, using the overview above as a reference.
- Invite the group to share initial responses to the readings, as well as any questions they may have.
- Ask for volunteers to share some of their daily responses from this week from *The Bible Year* devotional.
- If you are using *The Bible Year* videos, play the video for today's session now.
- Continue your discussion of the week's Bible passages with the questions below.

Discussion Questions

1. The father in Proverbs 4 is passing on wisdom his father taught him (vv. 1-9). What is the best wisdom those who raised you ever gave you? What's the most important piece of wisdom you'd like to pass on to young people today?
2. What's something your elders taught you that you definitely *wouldn't* pass on, and why?
3. Why do the sages devote such attention to warnings against adultery (5:1-23; 6:23-35; 7:1-27)? What other sins tend to arise from sexual infidelity?
4. Why and how do the sages use adultery as a metaphor for departure from God's ways more generally?

5. Why don't the sages warn about "loose men" as well as "loose women"? Does Proverbs reinforce negative stereotypes about women? Why or why not?
6. How do the proverbs find evidence of God's wisdom in the behavior of ants (6:6-11)? Where do you see such evidence in the created world? What evidence in nature would seem to contradict the sages' belief that God created an ordered world with predictable consequences?
7. Proverbs 8 draws a fascinating portrait of personified Wisdom. What do we learn about Wisdom's relationship to God and to humanity in this chapter? How might this view of Wisdom have influenced New Testament authors writing about Jesus (compare John 1:1-5; 1 Corinthians 1:26-31)?
8. Which of the proverbs in this week's chapters resonate most strongly with you, and why? Which ones, if any, do you have questions about or disagree with, and why?
9. Why does Proverbs devote such attention to what we say and how we say it (for example, in 12:16-26)? Do you have any personal rules for speaking in wise and godly ways?
10. While reading Proverbs, try memorizing at least one proverb you find meaningful each day. Tell others in your group why you memorized the proverbs you did.

Closing

+ Ask for several volunteers to summarize what they have found most meaningful about your discussion or about the biblical text this week. How might God be calling them to respond to it?
+ Invite the group to raise any prayer concerns or lift up any reasons for joy and thanksgiving.
+ Lead the group in a short closing prayer or invite a volunteer to do so.

Session 25

Proverbs 16:1–26:28

Overview

The proverbs of Solomon continue. The proverb form is admirably suited for memorable and poignant teaching, as well as for expressing stark and vivid contrasts between wisdom and folly, and even between God and mortals (examples: 16:2; 19:21; 20:24).

At Proverbs 22:17, Solomon's sayings give way to a collection of "sayings of the wise," which scholars note resembles a specific Egyptian wisdom text.[3] These sayings, like the preceding ones, urge trust in Israel's God (22:19; 24:21), who expects and enforces justice (22:22-23; 24:17-20).

After a few more "sayings of the wise" (24:23-34), we return to Solomon's proverbs, copied down by officials of righteous King Hezekiah (25:1). They sound by now familiar themes, including the value of prudent speech (25:11-20) and diligent work (26:13-16).

Another recurring concern in this week's chapters is how to conduct oneself properly before the king (16:13-15; 19:12; 20:2; 23:1-3; 25:6-7), suggesting the privileged social circles in which much Israelite wisdom was taught and heard, as well as reflecting its traditional associations with King Solomon.

Opening

- Begin with prayer.
- Invite a volunteer or volunteers to summarize the week's readings, using the overview above as a reference.
- Invite the group to share initial responses to the readings, as well as any questions they may have.
- Ask for volunteers to share some of their daily responses from this week from *The Bible Year* devotional.
- If you are using *The Bible Year* videos, play the video for today's session now.
- Continue your discussion of the week's Bible passages with the questions below.

Discussion Questions

1. Which of the proverbs in this week's chapters resonate most strongly with you, and why? Which ones, if any, do you have questions about or disagree with, and why?
2. What do you think about the way Proverbs 16:1-10 talks about God? How closely does it match what you believe about God?
3. Several proverbs in these chapters talk about gifts or bribes (17:8; 18:16; 21:14). What distinguishes the two? Do you think Proverbs is *describing* or *prescribing* using gifts to gain access to important people? Why?
4. Can Christians ever ethically use gifts or favors to achieve righteous ends? Why or why not?
5. As noted above, getting and staying in the king's good graces is a frequent concern in these chapters. For what reasons, if any, should God's people today seek the favor of powerful authorities?
6. How can we avoid succumbing to the temptation of valuing the trappings of power more than the reasons we sought access to it?

7. Proverbs extols the value of hard work (20:13; 24:30-34). How much have you benefited from working hard in your life? Is it reasonable to assume, as Proverbs does, that those who aren't well off haven't worked hard? Why or why not?
8. What does Proverbs' view of God as defender of those who are poor (22:22-23) suggest about how God's people today should act toward those in poverty?
9. Proverbs 23:29-35 warns against the dangers of "mixed wine." How like or unlike the sages' attitudes toward alcohol are your own? What resources for people who struggle with alcohol are in your community? How is your congregation one of those resources, or how might it be?

Closing

+ Ask for several volunteers to summarize what they have found most meaningful about your discussion or about the biblical text this week. How might God be calling them to respond to it?
+ Invite the group to raise any prayer concerns or lift up any reasons for joy and thanksgiving.
+ Lead the group in a short closing prayer or invite a volunteer to do so.

SESSION 26

Proverbs 27:1–
Ecclesiastes 12:14

Overview

Two collections of proverbs follow Solomon's further sayings.

The first, from an otherwise unknown man named Agur, sounds surprising notes of discouragement and humility compared with Proverbs' general attitude toward wisdom. Agur confesses his weariness and inability to comprehend God's ways (30:1-4)—as well as some ways of creatures and human beings (30:18-19)—but still asserts his confidence in God's truthful words (30:5-6).

The second, from an otherwise unknown King Lemuel, are the words of his mother. Lemuel's mother warns him against strong drink, lest he find himself incapable of delivering justice to people in poverty and distress (31:4-9); and extols the virtues of a "capable wife" who provides for her family, speaks wisdom, and honors God (31:10-31).

In stark contrast to Proverbs, the Teacher in Ecclesiastes laments the fleeting, futile nature of human existence and the utter inaccessibility of wisdom. Though he believes in God, the Teacher appears to doubt the ultimate justice other sages confidently promise. Faced with the inevitability of death for all, foolish and wise alike, the Teacher counsels enjoyment of the present and reverence for God as the hallmarks of a meaningful life.

Opening

- Begin with prayer.
- Invite a volunteer or volunteers to summarize the week's readings, using the overview above as a reference.
- Invite the group to share initial responses to the readings, as well as any questions they may have.
- Ask for volunteers to share some of their daily responses from this week from *The Bible Year* devotional.
- If you are using *The Bible Year* videos, play the video for today's session now.
- Continue your discussion of the week's Bible passages with the questions below.

Discussion Questions

1. Which of the proverbs in this week's chapters resonate most strongly with you, and why? Which ones, if any, do you have questions about or disagree with, and why?
2. King Lemuel's mother is the only identifiable woman author in Proverbs (though her words come to us through her son). Are you inspired or intimidated by the "competent wife" she describes in chapter 31? Should women today look to this woman as a role model? Why or why not?
3. How is the woman of Proverbs 31 like or unlike Woman Wisdom of Proverbs 8–9? Who are the wise women you and your congregation have blessed and praised (31:28)?
4. Throughout Ecclesiastes, the Teacher argues human life, brief and soon forgotten, "is an unhappy obsession" God gives us (1:13). Do you agree? Why or why not?

The Bible Year: Leader Guide

5. When have you felt you are "chasing after wind" (1:14)? How do you manage to find meaning when you feel this way?
6. The Teacher is disturbed by a lack of justice in this life and in whatever afterlife may await us (3:16–4:3). When have you been most disturbed by seeing or experiencing injustice? How have you responded? How can believing in a just afterlife motivate acting for justice now? How can it keep us from doing so?
7. What are the Teacher's attitudes toward youth and old age (11:7–12:8)? How do they compare to your own attitudes? What advantages do the young enjoy over the old? the old over the young? How specifically does your congregation help young and old to learn from each other?
8. How would you describe God as presented in Ecclesiastes? How do the Teacher's views of God confirm or challenge your own? How, if at all, does the gospel influence your approach to the Teacher's ideas about God?
9. Do you find the message of Ecclesiastes ultimately positive or negative, encouraging or discouraging? Why? What might God be saying through the Teacher to you and your congregation?

Closing

+ Ask for several volunteers to summarize what they have found most meaningful about your discussion or about the biblical text this week. How might God be calling them to respond to it?
+ Invite the group to raise any prayer concerns or lift up any reasons for joy and thanksgiving.
+ Lead the group in a short closing prayer or invite a volunteer to do so.

[Handwritten margin note: Ella – Ecc 3:1 – There is a season for everything. In those seasons you must trust & hold onto God – He'll lead you. We might thank its our season, but if it isn't God's!]

SESSION 27

Song of Solomon 1:1– Isaiah 23:18

Overview

In the Song of Solomon, also known as the Song of Songs, lovers often identified in tradition as King Solomon and one of his brides celebrate their physical and emotional intimacy in elaborate poetry. They and their community delight in each other's beauty and in their shared desire.

The prophet Isaiah of Jerusalem preached in Judah in the mid-eighth century BCE. He urged his nation to repent of its sins and trust in God, especially when threatened by foreign powers. When Israel (the Northern Kingdom) and Aram form an alliance against Judah, King Ahaz seeks an alliance with Assyria, the empire that Israel and Aram oppose. Isaiah insists God is using Assyria as an instrument of judgment against Israel and urges Ahaz to trust in God alone.

Isaiah's prophecy announces God's judgment of the nations surrounding Israel and Judah, as well as warnings of destruction for both the Northern and Southern Kingdoms (Israel and Judah) themselves. But it also offers promises of hope for the future. God promises remnants of both Israel and Judah will survive, and that Jerusalem will be restored and uplifted. God also promises a righteous king from David's line who will rule forever and a day when all nations will come to Mount Zion (that is, the Temple), to learn the ways of peace.

Opening

- Begin with prayer.
- Invite a volunteer or volunteers to summarize the week's readings, using the overview above as a reference.
- Invite the group to share initial responses to the readings, as well as any questions they may have.
- Ask for volunteers to share some of their daily responses from this week from *The Bible Year* devotional.
- If you are using *The Bible Year* videos, play the video for today's session now.
- Continue your discussion of the week's Bible passages with the questions below.

Discussion Questions

1. With the possible exception of 8:6 (depending upon one's translation),[4] the Song of Solomon (like Esther) doesn't mention God. Why is this extravagant and often overtly erotic love song in the Bible? What, if anything, does it suggest about God's will for romantic relationships?
2. Historically, many Jewish interpreters have read the Song as one about Israel's relationship with God, and many Christians have read it as one about Christ's love for the church, or for the individual believer. Do you find these interpretations helpful? Why or why not?
3. What is Isaiah's reaction to seeing God (6:1-5)? What message does God send Isaiah to proclaim (6:9-10)? How can we discern when God wants to send us with difficult messages? What do you learn from Isaiah's response in this passage?

4. For what specific sins does God pronounce judgment on Judah through Isaiah (1:16-17; 2:6-8; and 5:8-11, among others)? Would Isaiah recognize these sins in society today? What message might God bring to us, our society, and our church, through Isaiah?
5. Why does Isaiah reject King Ahaz's reluctance to ask for a sign (7:10-16)? What meaning does Isaiah want Ahaz to find in Immanuel's birth and childhood? Have you or your congregation ever faced a crisis that passed more quickly than you feared? How was God involved in that situation?
6. Isaiah 2:1-4 and 11:1-9 are vivid visions of a peaceful future. How will this peace encompass both the natural world and human society? How can and do these visions motivate God's people to act as peacemakers today?
7. Considering Israel's history as we've read it in the Bible, how do you react to Isaiah's prophecies in verses 19:18-25? What do these prophecies tell us about God? What practical implications, if any, do they have for relations between nations today?

Closing

- Ask for several volunteers to summarize what they have found most meaningful about your discussion or about the biblical text this week. How might God be calling them to respond to it?
- Invite the group to raise any prayer concerns or lift up any reasons for joy and thanksgiving.
- Lead the group in a short closing prayer or invite a volunteer to do so.

SESSION 28

Isaiah 24:1–52:12

Overview

Isaiah 24–27 anticipates God's imminent, decisive intervention in history. It involves catastrophic disaster and judgment of sinners (24:1-6; 26:20-21), but also the vindication of God's people (26:13-15) and the destruction of death for all peoples (25:6-9).

Isaiah 28–33 and 36–39 address the Assyrian threat to Judah during King Hezekiah's reign. Isaiah calls for trust in God rather than foreign alliances (28:14-16; 30:1-7; 31:1-3) and promises God's work of punishing the people for sin through Assyria will not last forever (30:18-26; 31:4-9).

In the late sixth century BCE, a "Second Isaiah" proclaimed a message of comfort and hope to Jewish exiles in Babylon (Isaiah 34–35; 40–55).

To those who fear God has abandoned God's people in the wake of Jerusalem's destruction and their time in Babylon, the prophet declares a new beginning. God anoints and empowers Persian emperor Cyrus (45:1) to be the one by whom God's people experience a second, even more miraculous exodus back to the Promised Land. God's saving acts demonstrate God is not just Israel's God but is the only God (44:6-8; 45:5-7), who sends a servant into the world on a special mission.

Isaiah 24:1–52:12

Opening

- Begin with prayer.
- Invite a volunteer or volunteers to summarize the week's readings, using the overview above as a reference.
- Invite the group to share initial responses to the readings, as well as any questions they may have.
- Ask for volunteers to share some of their daily responses from this week from *The Bible Year* devotional.
- If you are using *The Bible Year* videos, play the video for today's session now.
- Continue your discussion of the week's Bible passages with the questions below.

Discussion Questions

1. How does Isaiah 24–27 envision a future in which God's triumph is absolute and undeniable? What enemies will God defeat? What effects do God's victories have? What "other masters" have ruled or try to rule over you, and what do you do to "profess [God's] name alone" instead (26:13)?

2. Isaiah describes God's use of the Assyrian siege of Jerusalem to judge Judah as a "strange" deed (28:21). What "strange" deeds have you seen or experienced God doing in the world or in your life? What criteria do or ought God's people use to identify such "strange" works? How cautious or confident ought we be, and why?

3. Although Second Isaiah uses Exodus imagery to describe the return from Babylon, he also says God wants the people to focus not on "the prior things" that they may see God's "new thing" (read 43:16-21). When, if ever, has your or your congregation's remembrance of God's past deeds made it harder to discern new things God was doing?

4. How do we balance memory of our past with God and openness to a new and different future with God?
5. God calls Cyrus "anointed"—in Hebrew, *messiah* (45:1). Why? What other people have you read about in the Bible this year who act as "messiahs," even if they don't bear that title?
6. Israel's kings were called anointed ("messiah") and other rulers like Cyrus were described in this way as well. Why do Christians distinguish Jesus as Messiah apart from other "messiahs" in Scripture?
7. Three of four "Servant Songs" in Second Isaiah appear in this week's reading: verses 42:1-4; 49:1-6; and 50:4-9. Read, compare, and contrast these Scriptures. What do they tell us about the Servant's identity and mission? What insights might they offer your congregation and you as you strive to serve God today?

Closing

+ Ask for several volunteers to summarize what they have found most meaningful about your discussion or about the biblical text this week. How might God be calling them to respond to it?
+ Invite the group to raise any prayer concerns or lift up any reasons for joy and thanksgiving.
+ Lead the group in a short closing prayer or invite a volunteer to do so.

SESSION 29

Isaiah 52:13–Jeremiah 16:21

Overview

Isaiah 52:13–53:12 is the last of the four "Servant Songs" in Second Isaiah. It describes how God's servant unjustly suffers rejection, pain, and death as an offering for the people's sin. His suffering makes many righteous, and God promises to vindicate the servant.

Isaiah 56–66, like the apocalyptic vision of Isaiah 24–27, seems to address the situation the exiles who returned from Babylon faced in Jerusalem. The prophet accuses the people of idolatry and social injustices that keep them from experiencing the prosperity and blessing God had promised. God announces punishment for those who persist in rebellion against God, but salvation for those who repent and remain faithful, and the creation of "a new heaven and a new earth" (65:17).

Active during Babylon's threats to and eventual conquest of Judah, the prophet Jeremiah calls on the people to cease their sinful and unjust ways, and renew their devotion to God. He reacts to the coming destruction and exile with horror and grief. But neither his forceful preaching (for example, 7:1-15) nor his symbolic actions—burying and retrieving a linen loincloth (13:1-11), his celibacy (16:1-4)—gain his message a hearing.

Opening

- Begin with prayer.
- Invite a volunteer or volunteers to summarize the week's readings, using the overview above as a reference.
- Invite the group to share initial responses to the readings, as well as any questions they may have.
- Ask for volunteers to share some of their daily responses from this week from *The Bible Year* devotional.
- If you are using *The Bible Year* videos, play the video for today's session now.
- Continue your discussion of the week's Bible passages with the questions below.

Discussion Questions

1. Because early Christians relied on Isaiah's fourth "Servant Song" to understand Jesus's death and resurrection, Christians today often find reading it as anything but a direct prediction of Jesus difficult. How might the Jews who'd lived through the Babylonian Exile have understood Isaiah's words, especially if the nation itself is the Servant? What do you think about God making the Servant suffer for other people's sins?
2. What is wrong with worship in the post-Exile community, according to Isaiah 58? What about the worship of God's people before the Exile, according to Jeremiah 7:1-15? How do you and your congregation demonstrate integrity between who you are in worship and at other times?
3. Prophets in the Bible often initially object to God's call. What objections does Jeremiah raise to God's call of him, and how does God answer these objections (1:4-10)?

4. When, if ever, have you felt ill-equipped to say or do something God wanted you to say or do? How did God respond? What happened?
5. Readers sometimes call Jeremiah "the weeping prophet," in part, for his outbursts of sorrow over Judah's sin and its consequences (examples: 4:19-22; 8:18–9:3).[5] Has there been a time when others' unrighteousness has moved you to tears? If so, what did you do about it? To what extent do you think Jeremiah's sorrow reflects God's own, and why?
6. What are Jeremiah's complaints about his prophetic mission, and how does God respond (11:18–12:6)? Why did Jeremiah's message inspire such opposition? Are there prophets today who meet resistance for speaking God's truth? If so, who?
7. How is Jeremiah's message different from what other prophets are preaching to the people (14:13-18)? How do we discern whether those who claim to speak for God actually are, or are simply telling us what we want to hear?

Closing

- Ask for several volunteers to summarize what they have found most meaningful about your discussion or about the biblical text this week. How might God be calling them to respond to it?
- Invite the group to raise any prayer concerns or lift up any reasons for joy and thanksgiving.
- Lead the group in a short closing prayer or invite a volunteer to do so.

SESSION 30

Jeremiah 17:1–49:39

Overview

Despite his own deep reluctance—even his feelings that God has forced him into his prophetic role—Jeremiah continues to denounce Judah's idolatry and social injustice. Yet he continues to meet opposition. His preaching in the Temple almost results in the priests and the royal court sentencing him to death. At one point, the priests even throw him in a well ("a cistern," 37:36) and leave him to die. But Jeremiah cannot contain the message God gives.

When Babylon's armies besiege Jerusalem and deport most of its people, Jeremiah writes a letter telling the exiles to build lives for themselves in Babylon, for their exile will not end soon. But he also looks ahead to the exiles' return. When God's time is fulfilled, God will bring the people back, raise up a righteous king from David's line to rule them, and will radically renew the covenant with them, placing divine law directly in their hearts.

After Jerusalem falls, Jeremiah tells survivors not to go to Egypt as they plan. They go anyway, taking Jeremiah with them. There, he continues to prophesy, announcing God will judge Egypt and many surrounding nations as well, and condemning the survivors of Judah for their ongoing idolatry.

Jeremiah 17:1–49:39

Opening

- Begin with prayer.
- Invite a volunteer or volunteers to summarize the week's readings, using the overview above as a reference.
- Invite the group to share initial responses to the readings, as well as any questions they may have.
- Ask for volunteers to share some of their daily responses from this week from *The Bible Year* devotional.
- If you are using *The Bible Year* videos, play the video for today's session now.
- Continue your discussion of the week's Bible passages with the questions below.

Discussion Questions

1. Jeremiah preaches against the people's failure to observe the Sabbath (17:19-27). Why are these Sabbath violations such a serious matter?
2. What does observing the Sabbath look like for modern Christians? How well do you and your congregation keep it?
3. What is the deeper significance of Jeremiah's visit to the potter's house (18:1-11)? Do you think God uses nations in this way today? Do you think God actively shapes evil against God's people (v. 11)? Why or why not?
4. What criticisms does Jeremiah level against King Josiah's sons who succeed him (22:11-23)? How are they failing to follow in their father's footsteps?
5. How and why does feeling "safe and secure" (22:21) tempt the prosperous—not just monarchs—to stop listening to God? How can and does the church encourage those who are "safe and secure" to keep listening to and obeying God?

The Bible Year: Leader Guide

6. When the priests and official prophets want to sentence Jeremiah to death for his preaching, other officials and the people intervene (26:1-19). What precedent do they invoke for sparing Jeremiah? When was a time you or your congregation were able to hear an unpopular or upsetting message as a word from God? What happened as a result?
7. In his letter to the exiles, Jeremiah tells them to "promote the welfare" of the place God has sent them (29:7). How did he tell them to do this? What, specifically, are you and your congregation doing to "promote the welfare" of your city or community?
8. Scholars often call Jeremiah 30–33 "the little book of consolation."[6] What consoling and comforting message do these chapters contain for the exiles? for you and your congregation?
9. How does the "new covenant" God promises the people in Jeremiah 31:31-34 differ from the previous covenant? What would life look like in a world where all people knew God?

Closing

+ Ask for several volunteers to summarize what they have found most meaningful about your discussion or about the biblical text this week. How might God be calling them to respond to it?
+ Invite the group to raise any prayer concerns or lift up any reasons for joy and thanksgiving.
+ Lead the group in a short closing prayer or invite a volunteer to do so.

SESSION 31

Jeremiah 50:1– Ezekiel 21:32

Overview

Although Jeremiah conveys God's promise to judge Babylon, the book ends with an account of Jerusalem's fall, the Temple's destruction, and the deportation of the exiles. Like 2 Kings, Jeremiah ends with notice of King Jehoiachin's favored treatment in Babylon.

The Book of Lamentations grieves the devastation Jerusalem has endured at the hands of Babylon and of God. It acknowledges Judah's sins and voices horror at their consequences. It pleads for divine mercy and expresses confidence in God's faithful love.

Ezekiel is a priest who was among the population Babylon deported from Judah. In Babylon, he has visions of God's glory, which has departed the Temple in Jerusalem where it once dwelled but is now in Babylon, with God's exiled people. Ezekiel performs symbolic actions to communicate the meaning of Jerusalem's siege and fall. He calls the people to repent of idolatry. He also conveys God's promise to remember the everlasting covenant with Israel and forgive the people's sins, gathering them again to Mount Zion from the lands where they have been scattered.

Opening

- Begin with prayer.
- Invite a volunteer or volunteers to summarize the week's readings, using the overview above as a reference.
- Invite the group to share initial responses to the readings, as well as any questions they may have.
- Ask for volunteers to share some of their daily responses from this week from *The Bible Year* devotional.
- If you are using *The Bible Year* videos, play the video for today's session now.
- Continue your discussion of the week's Bible passages with the questions below.

Discussion Questions

1. Lamentations is a highly structured series of acrostic poems in Hebrew—raw and real emotions, cast in careful artistic form. When and how does art, of any kind, help you express your feelings to God?
2. How does your congregation value the way poets, musicians, painters, and other artists can help God's people pray?
3. Lamentations describes God's judgment of Judah in vivid ways. Which ones struck you most as you read, and why? How easy or difficult do you imagine it was for the poet to affirm God's love and mercy (3:22-24) in the midst of such desolation?
4. When do you find it hard to see God's mercies, and what do you in situations like this?
5. In Ezekiel 1, why does the prophet so often describe the divine chariot he sees in approximate terms—"looked like," "were like," "was like"? Why does he emphasize its motion (1:14-24)? How is the fact Ezekiel sees God's glory among his fellow exiles in Babylon a cause for both sorrow and hope (see also Ezekiel 10)?

6. What does Ezekiel do to symbolically "act out" Babylon's siege and attack of Jerusalem (chapters 4–5)? Why do you think God commanded him to do these things?
7. What's the strangest, most memorable, or most dramatic thing you've ever seen someone do—or that you have done—to try and communicate God's message?
8. How do you react to the metaphorical depiction of God and Israel's relationship in Ezekiel 16? How might women who have been abused, and the men who have abused them, hear this Scripture? How might this chapter communicate God's word today?
9. In Ezekiel 18:25-32, what is God's answer to those who question the fairness of God's ways? What do you think about this response? What "unfair ways" you see in our society that lead to death rather than life? How can God's people show society that God takes no pleasure in anyone's death (v. 32)?

Closing

- Ask for several volunteers to summarize what they have found most meaningful about your discussion or about the biblical text this week. How might God be calling them to respond to it?
- Invite the group to raise any prayer concerns or lift up any reasons for joy and thanksgiving.
- Lead the group in a short closing prayer or invite a volunteer to do so.

SESSION 32

Ezekiel 22:1– Daniel 6:28

Overview

God calls Ezekiel a "lookout" (33:7; see also 3:17), commanded to warn God's people of their sin's consequences. The prophet repeatedly and forcefully does so. Even the death of his wife becomes an occasion to prophesy. Although the people do not repent, God holds Ezekiel guiltless because he faithfully proclaims God's message.

After Jerusalem's destruction, God's message through Ezekiel sounds increasingly hopeful. God promises to gather the people as a shepherd gathers his flock, and grants Ezekiel a vision of dry bones given new flesh and breath—an image of the nation restored to life in the land. Ezekiel's prophecy culminates in a vision of God's victory over the mighty and mysterious Gog and of a new temple to which God's glorious presence returns, from which a life-giving river flows and in which God's holy priests and people worship.

The first six chapters of Daniel contain narratives about Daniel and his companions in Babylon. Like Ezekiel, Daniel lives in Babylon during the Exile. He is one of four young elites taken to live in the court. Though given Babylonian names, they remain true to God's law. Daniel's three friends—Shadrach, Meshach, and Abednego—miraculously survive being thrown into a fiery furnace for refusing to worship the king's golden statue.

Daniel interprets dreams and visions for the king, whose advisors' conspiracy against Daniel lands him a den of lions. But Daniel, too, survives, protected by the God to whom he remains faithful.

Opening

- Begin with prayer.
- Invite a volunteer or volunteers to summarize the week's readings, using the overview above as a reference.
- Invite the group to share initial responses to the readings, as well as any questions they may have.
- Ask for volunteers to share some of their daily responses from this week from *The Bible Year* devotional.
- If you are using *The Bible Year* videos, play the video for today's session now.
- Continue your discussion of the week's Bible passages with the questions below.

Discussion Questions

1. Against which nations other than Judah does Ezekiel pronounce God's judgment, and why (chapters 25–32)? Do the prophet's warnings resonate in relevant ways for nations today, including your own? Why or why not?
2. How does Ezekiel's vision of the dry bones communicate hope to the exiles in Babylon (37:1-14)? How have you seen or experienced God's Word and "breath" (v. 9) bring new life to a community that considered itself, or was considered by others, dead (v. 11)?
3. Why does Ezekiel's vision of the people's restoration focus on a new Temple (43:1-12)? To what extent should Ezekiel's exacting attention to the new temple guide Christians as we make physical or figurative space for God's holy presence in the world and in our lives?

The Bible Year: Leader Guide

4. When Daniel and his three friends are taken to the Babylonian court, they receive new names and face pressure to conform to new standards of diet and education (1:3-7). Have you ever actively resisted specific cultural norms and expectations you believed contradicted God's commands or God's will for you? What happened?
5. How do you discern when you must resist to maintain your distinctive identity as one who belongs to God?
6. After Shadrach, Meshach, and Abednego survive the fiery furnace and Daniel survives the lion's den, the rulers of Babylon officially recognize the God of Israel's power and authority (3:28-29; 6:25-27). Who do you know or know of whose example of godly integrity inspired others, especially people in positions of power, to honor God?

Closing

+ Ask for several volunteers to summarize what they have found most meaningful about your discussion or about the biblical text this week. How might God be calling them to respond to it?
+ Invite the group to raise any prayer concerns or lift up any reasons for joy and thanksgiving.
+ Lead the group in a short closing prayer or invite a volunteer to do so.

SESSION 33

Daniel 7:1 –Amos 9:15

Overview

Daniel experiences several startling visions in chapters 7–12. He sees destructive beasts rise from the sea to be judged and destroyed by God, who gives authority to one "like a human being" from heaven (7:13). He sees conflicts between kings on earth that mirror angelic warfare in heaven. He sees the angel Gabriel tell him when God's people are finally saved, many who are dead will rise—some to "eternal life" and others to "eternal disgrace" (12:2).

Hosea is the first of the twelve minor prophets. The prophet Hosea preached a message of God's persistent love for God's rebellious people in the Northern Kingdom in the mid-eighth century BCE. Hosea enacted the message God gave him by marrying a prostitute named Gomer. Hosea's broken marriage symbolizes Israel's broken covenant with God. As Hosea shames but then woos Gomer back, so will God punish and woo back Israel, unable to destroy Israel in anger.

The prophet Joel interpreted swarming locusts, drought, and fires in fifth-century BCE Judah as God's summons for the nation to repent. Joel announces God will be gracious and will pour out the divine spirit on all the people.

The prophet Amos was tending livestock and trees in Judah when God called him to preach in the Northern Kingdom, Israel, in the mid-eighth century BCE. Amos denounces the nation's persistent social injustices and foretells a grim day of reckoning drawing near.

Opening

- Begin with prayer.
- Invite a volunteer or volunteers to summarize the week's readings, using the overview above as a reference.
- Invite the group to share initial responses to the readings, as well as any questions they may have.
- Ask for volunteers to share some of their daily responses from this week from *The Bible Year* devotional.
- If you are using *The Bible Year* videos, play the video for today's session now.
- Continue your discussion of the week's Bible passages with the questions below.

Discussion Questions

1. Scholars believe many of Daniel's visions refer to history not otherwise found in Jewish and Protestant Bibles, including the rise of Alexander the Great (11:3-4; died 323 BCE), and the tyranny of Antiochus IV Epiphanes (11:21-45), against whom the Maccabees rebelled (167-160 BCE).[7] How might these chapters have encouraged Jews during the expansion of Greek power and culture across the ancient world?

2. What encouragement do the visions of Daniel 7–12 offer God's people as the modern world faces powerful, sweeping changes? Do you believe God is directing human history toward a specific goal? Why or why not?

3. What do you think about Hosea's marriage to and children with Gomer (chapters 1-3)? Does its significance as an allegory of God's relationship

with Israel justify Hosea's harsh language about and treatment of Gomer—or of the faithful partner in a relationship repeatedly taking back one who is unfaithful? What positive lessons can we learn from their relationship?

4. Joel calls the people of Judah to repent in the face of ecological disasters (chapter 1). Do you think the ecological disasters we face are a summons to repent? If so, of what, and what forms should that repentance take? If not, why not?

5. For what specific sins does God indict Israel through Amos's preaching (for example, 5:6-12; 6:1-8)? How does identifying these sins give substance to Amos's well-known call for "ever-flowing" justice and righteousness (5:24)?

6. What would a rolling stream of justice look like in our society? What are you and your congregation doing to help it flow?

7. Why is the priest Amaziah angry at Amos (7:10-17)? What is Amos's response? What are the potential risks and rewards of communicating God's message beyond your "home turf," as Amos did? How do we discern when we should or should not do so?

Closing

+ Ask for several volunteers to summarize what they have found most meaningful about your discussion or about the biblical text this week. How might God be calling them to respond to it?
+ Invite the group to raise any prayer concerns or lift up any reasons for joy and thanksgiving.
+ Lead the group in a short closing prayer or invite a volunteer to do so.

SESSION 34

Obadiah–
Habakkuk 3:19

Overview

Obadiah chastises the Edomites—descendants of Esau (Genesis 25:30)—for taking advantage of Jerusalem after its fall to Babylon. He foretells divine retribution, and a day when Israelites will again possess the land and no Edomites will survive.

The Book of Jonah tells how God calls Jonah to go preach against Nineveh, Babylon's capital. Jonah initially disobeys, but after a stormy sea voyage and time in a big fish's belly, he goes, announcing the wicked city will be overthrown. When all Nineveh, from king to cattle, repent in sackcloth and ashes, God relents and does not bring destruction on them. Jonah finds God's mercy infuriating.

In the eighth century BCE, Micah proclaims God's impending judgment against both the Northern and Southern Kingdoms for the injustice and violence in their societies. He also declares God's future compassion, speaking of God's restored people on Mount Zion and a king from Bethlehem who will be raised up to govern the people in peace.

In the late seventh century BCE, Nahum attributes Babylon's defeat of Assyria to God, and exults over its destruction, promising Judah the wicked will never invade.

Around the turn of the sixth century BCE, Habakkuk asks timeless questions about why evil prospers. God promises justice, even if it appears slow in coming. The prophet resolves to praise God even in times of trouble.

Opening

- Begin with prayer.
- Invite a volunteer or volunteers to summarize the week's readings, using the overview above as a reference.
- Invite the group to share initial responses to the readings, as well as any questions they may have.
- Ask for volunteers to share some of their daily responses from this week from *The Bible Year* devotional.
- If you are using *The Bible Year* videos, play the video for today's session now.
- Continue your discussion of the week's Bible passages with the questions below.

Discussion Questions

1. How does Obadiah's prophecy reflect the ancient family feud between Jacob and Esau (see Genesis 25–27, 32–33)? How have you seen or experienced old conflicts you thought resolved erupt again?
2. What work must be done to ensure long-standing hurts between people, between communities, and between nations can be healed?
3. Why does Jonah not want to go preach in Nineveh (4:1-2)? What does Jonah's story suggest about our ability to avoid doing what God would have us do? About the nature and importance of repentance?
4. When have you experienced frustration or anger when God deals mercifully with those we may not think deserve mercy?

5. After three days and nights in the stomach of the big fish but before the fish vomits him onto dry land, Jonah prays a psalm of thanksgiving to God (2:1-10). When's a time you were in "the belly of the beast"? How, if at all, did you pray to God during that experience? How could Jonah's psalm be a model for you the next time you're swallowed in darkness?
6. What does God require of human beings, according to Micah 6:6-8? How does Micah say Israel and Judah fall short of these requirements (examples: 2:1-3; 3:1-12; 7:2-6)? In what specific ways are you and your congregation meeting them? How can the church best communicate these requirements to society today?
7. Nahum declares "the worthless one will never again invade" Judah (1:15)—about two decades before Babylon conquers Jerusalem. Should people of faith read Nahum's prophecy today? Why or why not?
8. What has ever moved you to ask God, "How long?" as Habakkuk does? How have you waited (or are you waiting) for God to answer? How do you believe God has answered you?

Closing

+ Ask for several volunteers to summarize what they have found most meaningful about your discussion or about the biblical text this week. How might God be calling them to respond to it?
+ Invite the group to raise any prayer concerns or lift up any reasons for joy and thanksgiving.
+ Lead the group in a short closing prayer or invite a volunteer to do so.

SESSION 35

Zephaniah 1:1– Malachi 4:6

Overview

During the reign of King Josiah, Zephaniah announces God's judgment of Judah and its enemies for their sins. He anticipates imminent and total destruction, which he urges the "humble of the land" (2:3) to try to avoid by righteous living, but also a future in which God dwells in Jerusalem with the gathered and restored people.

Haggai calls on those who have returned from exile in Babylon to begin rebuilding the Temple. Under the leadership of Zerubbabel their governor and Joshua their priest, they do. God promises to make the new Temple as glorious as the old by shaking treasure for it from the nations.

Around the same time Haggai is active, Zechariah has visions encouraging Joshua and Zerubbabel, God's anointed leaders, in their work. He also looks forward to the Branch, a messiah of David's house who is yet to come, and to a day when all nations will come to Jerusalem seeking God's favor.

Malachi speaks God's judgment against corruption in the Temple priesthood, as well as the people's failure to give their full tithe. He announces the coming of a messenger from God who will purify the priests, as well as the return of the prophet Elijah before the day God will burn up the wicked and save the righteous.

Opening

- Begin with prayer.
- Invite a volunteer or volunteers to summarize the week's readings, using the overview above as a reference.
- Invite the group to share initial responses to the readings, as well as any questions they may have.
- Ask for volunteers to share some of their daily responses from this week from *The Bible Year* devotional.
- If you are using *The Bible Year* videos, play the video for today's session now.
- Continue your discussion of the week's Bible passages with the questions below.

Discussion Questions

1. What charges does Zephaniah level against the powerful and elite in Jerusalem (3:3-4)? How does he describe the remnant of the people who will survive God's judgment (3:12-13)? What does this contrast show us about God's values and priorities, and how they shape our own?
2. Back in 2 Samuel 7, God wasn't concerned about having a nice Temple. In Haggai, however, God wants the people to rebuild the Temple (1:2-11) and promises to make it glorious (2:3-9). Why is having a glorious dwelling for God a more urgent priority in Haggai's day than in David's?
3. What does a community's attitude toward its sacred space reveal about its attitude toward God? How do we know when our sacred spaces have become more important to us than God?

4. In one of his visions, Zechariah sees the priest Joshua's dirty clothing replaced with festival attire (3:1-5). What does this wardrobe change represent? When have you felt God has replaced your "dirty laundry" with clean garments? What do you do to try to avoid getting filthy again?
5. Zechariah sees a day when old and young will live safely in Jerusalem's streets (8:1-8). When you consider the streets of your own city, does such a vision seem impossible to you? Why or why not?
6. How can and do people of faith work to make city streets safe places for old people to sit and for children to play?
7. What does Zechariah's announcement of the king to come (9:9-10) suggest about the qualities most important in rulers and authorities? Why did Jesus's earliest followers interpret this prophecy as one about him?
8. According to Malachi, what are the ethical implications for people who believe God is the "father" of all (2:10-12)? How does your congregation live out those implications today, both within and beyond its own membership?

Closing

- Ask for several volunteers to summarize what they have found most meaningful about your discussion or about the biblical text this week. How might God be calling them to respond to it?
- Invite the group to raise any prayer concerns or lift up any reasons for joy and thanksgiving.
- Lead the group in a short closing prayer or invite a volunteer to do so.

SESSION 36

Matthew 1:1–12:50

Overview

Matthew begins his account of Jesus the Messiah by tracing Jesus's genealogy from Abraham, through King David, and ultimately to Joseph, husband of Mary, Jesus's mother. Though born in Bethlehem, Jesus is raised in Nazareth, where his family makes its home after living in Egypt to protect him from murderous Herod, king of Judea.

As an adult, Jesus is baptized by John the Baptist. After forty days of temptation in the wilderness, and after John is arrested by Herod Antipas (King Herod the Great's son), Jesus begins a public ministry in the Galilee region of preaching, teaching, and performing miracles.

Jesus proclaims the kingdom of heaven's nearness and interprets Torah for his disciples so they can be a community ready to live in it. He insists he has come not to end God's Law but to fulfill it. He calls his followers to greater observance than even the sect of the Pharisees by emphasizing the core principles of God's commands.

From prison, John sends messengers to ask Jesus if Jesus is the Messiah. In reply, Jesus points to his miracles and his proclamation of good news to those in poverty. The author of Matthew quotes and applies Scripture to Jesus throughout his Gospel, making it clear he believes Jesus is the one for whom John and Israel have waited.

Matthew 1:1–12:50

Opening

- Begin with prayer.
- Invite a volunteer or volunteers to summarize the week's readings, using the overview above as a reference.
- Invite the group to share initial responses to the readings, as well as any questions they may have.
- Ask for volunteers to share some of their daily responses from this week from *The Bible Year* devotional.
- If you are using *The Bible Year* videos, play the video for today's session now.
- Continue your discussion of the week's Bible passages with the questions below.

Discussion Questions

1. What do we learn about Jesus from Matthew's genealogy of him (chapter 1)? Which names do you recognize, and what part did they play in God's history with Israel and the world? Why do you think Matthew begins his account of Jesus with this family tree?
2. Matthew *tells* us Joseph is "a righteous man" (1:19), but how does he also *show* us (chapters 1–2)? Have any men in your life who are not your biological father been father figures to you? If so, how?
3. What qualities may make Joseph a role model for men today? Could Joseph also be a role model for women? How?
4. Why is Herod, the king the Roman Empire has installed in Judea, so alarmed by the news of Jesus's birth—alarmed enough to slaughter innocent children (2:1-18)? How does the kingdom of heaven the adult Jesus preaches in Matthew 5–7 contrast with and challenge earthly kingdoms and those who rule them?

5. As narrator, Matthew often quotes Scripture (in this week's verses: 1:23; 2:15, 17-18, 23; 3:3; 4:14-16; 12:17-21), as does Jesus (see for example: 4:1-11; 5:21-48). How does this reliance on Scripture connect God's past activity to what God is doing in Jesus's life? Why do these connections matter—for Matthew, and for Christians today?
6. Do you understand Jesus's Beatitudes (5:1-12) as *prescriptive*—telling people what to do—or *descriptive*, or in some other way? Why? Which one speaks most powerfully to you?
7. When, if ever, have you asked John's question of Jesus (11:2-3)? If someone were to "Go, report" what they "hear and see" (v. 4) about your congregation, what would they have heard and seen of Jesus's activity?

Closing

- Ask for several volunteers to summarize what they have found most meaningful about your discussion or about the biblical text this week. How might God be calling them to respond to it?
- Invite the group to raise any prayer concerns or lift up any reasons for joy and thanksgiving.
- Lead the group in a short closing prayer or invite a volunteer to do so.

Session 37

Matthew 13:1–25:46

Overview

Jesus preaches about the kingdom of heaven using parables. Rejected in Nazareth but followed elsewhere by crowds thousands strong, Jesus miraculously feeds the people with a few loaves and fish. He walks across the Sea of Galilee in a storm to join his disciples in a boat so they may minister on the sea's far shore.

Some religious leaders of various groups question and oppose Jesus: members of the Pharisees (a sect characterized by meticulous observance of Jewish Law), the Sadducees (a sect that, among other things, did not look for future resurrection of the dead), and scribes (expert interpreters of Torah). Jesus defends his teaching and accuses his opponents of hypocrisy.

Jesus's disciple Simon Peter confesses Jesus as Messiah, but rebukes him when Jesus talks of his own imminent suffering, death, and resurrection. Jesus rebukes Peter, teaching that his disciples must voluntarily suffer to follow him. Peter, James, and John see Jesus speaking in glory with Moses and Elijah on a mountain, after which Jesus teaches them those who are like children are greatest in the kingdom of heaven.

Jesus goes to Jerusalem with his disciples to celebrate Passover. He disputes with and denounces religious leaders who oppose him, foretells the Temple's destruction, and tells parables about the coming of "the Son of Man" in the messianic age.

Opening

- Begin with prayer.
- Invite a volunteer or volunteers to summarize the week's readings, using the overview above as a reference.
- Invite the group to share initial responses to the readings, as well as any questions they may have.
- Ask for volunteers to share some of their daily responses from this week from *The Bible Year* devotional.
- If you are using *The Bible Year* videos, play the video for today's session now.
- Continue your discussion of the week's Bible passages with the questions below.

Discussion Questions

1. Why does Jesus teach using parables (13:13-15, 34-35)? Which of Jesus's parables of the kingdom in Matthew 13 most appeals to or intrigues you? Which most confuses or frustrates you? Why?
2. Based on Jesus's parables, what adjectives would you use to describe the kingdom of heaven?
3. Why does Jesus treat the Canaanite mother as he does (15:23-26)? How does the woman prevail upon him to help her daughter? What, if anything, does this encounter teach us about treating people who are "other"?
4. Only Matthew records Jesus's promise to Peter about building the church "on this rock" (16:18-19). What does Jesus mean? What more does he say about the church in verses 18:15-22? What issues might have been important to Matthew's church, based on these passages? Are the same issues important to yours? Why or why not?

5. What is surprising about Jesus's parable of the landowner and vineyard workers (20:1-16)? How is this story like the kingdom of heaven? When have you felt like the grumbling workers (vv. 11-12)? Would (or do) others grumble at you because of your generosity?
6. Jesus is at odds with Pharisees in all the Gospels, but his "woes" (see NRSV) against them in Matthew 23 are especially harsh. Jesus and his followers were Jews. To what extent does this chapter reflect a heated "family argument" about faith between Jesus's earliest followers and other Jews in the first century? To what extent does it reflect actual hypocrisy—and when have you been guilty of similar hypocrisies yourself?
7. By what criteria will the King who comes judge the nations (25:31-46; compare 7:21-23)? How does Jesus's story about the future shape your and your congregation's actions today?

Closing

- Ask for several volunteers to summarize what they have found most meaningful about your discussion or about the biblical text this week. How might God be calling them to respond to it?
- Invite the group to raise any prayer concerns or lift up any reasons for joy and thanksgiving.
- Lead the group in a short closing prayer or invite a volunteer to do so.

SESSION 38

Matthew 26:1 –Mark 10:45

Overview

Judas betrays Jesus to the chief priests after celebrating Passover with Jesus and the other apostles. He later takes his own life.

As Jesus stands trial, Peter three times denies knowing him. Pilate, Roman governor of Judea, refuses to release Jesus when Jesus is brought before him. Jesus is crucified but raised. He sends the remaining eleven disciples to teach and baptize people of all nations, promising to be with them forever.

Mark begins his Gospel with the preaching of John the baptizer, who baptizes Jesus. After forty days' temptation in the wilderness and after John is arrested, Jesus begins a public ministry in the Galilee region of preaching, teaching, and performing miracles. He chooses twelve apostles to proclaim repentance, cast out demons, and heal. Rejected in Nazareth—his own family seeks to restrain him—Jesus is followed by crowds thousands strong, whom he miraculously feeds with a few loaves and two fish.

Peter confesses Jesus as Messiah, but rebukes him when Jesus talks of his own imminent suffering, death, and resurrection. Jesus rebukes Peter, teaching that his disciples must voluntarily suffer to follow him. Peter, James, and John see Jesus speaking in glory with Elijah and Moses on a mountain.

Opening

- Begin with prayer.
- Invite a volunteer or volunteers to summarize the week's readings, using the overview above as a reference.
- Invite the group to share initial responses to the readings, as well as any questions they may have.
- Ask for volunteers to share some of their daily responses from this week from *The Bible Year* devotional.
- If you are using *The Bible Year* videos, play the video for today's session now.
- Continue your discussion of the week's Bible passages with the questions below.

Discussion Questions

1. Only Matthew records Judas's death by suicide and the fate of the silver pieces (27:3-10). Why is Matthew interested in this event? Do you think Jesus, after his resurrection, would have forgiven Judas had Judas repented to him? Why? How does your congregation help people struggling with suicidal thoughts? *NOTE: In the US, the 24/7 National Suicide Prevention Lifeline is 1-800-273-8255.*

2. For centuries, Christians have abused Matthew's unique assignment of blame for Jesus's death (27:24-25) to justify anti-Jewish hatred and violence. Matthew understood Jesus's death as the reason Rome destroyed Jerusalem in 70 CE during a Jewish revolt. How should Christians understand this "blood libel" today?

3. Only in Matthew do Jewish leaders conspire to cover up Jesus's resurrection (27:62-66; 28:11-15). How

would Matthew's original readers, at odds with their synagogues because of their faith, have understood these passages? How should modern Christians read them?
4. How do people with religious and political power today attempt to hold on to it in the face of God's power to give new life?
5. Where is Jesus at the end of Matthew? What implications does Matthew's ending have for Jesus's church today?
6. Jesus's command against revealing his identity as Messiah is not strictly unique to Mark (Matthew 16:20) but is a notable theme (Mark 1:25, 34, 43-44; 3:17; 5:43; 7:36; 8:26, 30; 9:9). What do you make of Jesus's "messianic secret"?
7. Based on your reading of Matthew and, to this point, Mark, why do you think the church did not choose one Gospel over the other, but kept both?

Closing

- Ask for several volunteers to summarize what they have found most meaningful about your discussion or about the biblical text this week. How might God be calling them to respond to it?
- Invite the group to raise any prayer concerns or lift up any reasons for joy and thanksgiving.
- Lead the group in a short closing prayer or invite a volunteer to do so.

SESSION 39

Mark 10:46 –Luke 4:13

Overview

Jesus enters Jerusalem, where he disputes with religious leaders who oppose him and he foretells the Temple's destruction and the coming of "the Human One" in the messianic age. Betrayed by Judas and denied by Peter, Jesus is crucified and buried. When three women go to his tomb, they discover it unsealed. A young man tells them Jesus has been raised. The women flee from the tomb, terrified. In what was likely Mark's original ending, they tell no one.

Luke begins his "carefully account" (1:3) of Jesus's life by relating the miraculous conception and birth of John the Baptist to his elderly parents, the priest Zechariah and Elizabeth. Elizabeth's relative Mary is told she will also conceive, though she is a virgin.

When the Roman emperor declares a census, Mary and Joseph, to whom she is engaged, travel from Nazareth to Joseph's ancestral town of Bethlehem, where she gives birth to Jesus. Angels announce Jesus's birth to shepherds.

When Mary and Joseph present their infant in the Temple in Jerusalem, the prophets Simeon and Anna proclaim the child's importance.

When he is twelve, Jesus stays behind in the Temple after a festival, engaged in precocious discussion with teachers of the Law.

About thirty years later, a grown John baptizes his relative Jesus, who then endures forty days' temptation in the wilderness.

Opening

- Begin with prayer.
- Invite a volunteer or volunteers to summarize the week's readings, using the overview above as a reference.
- Invite the group to share initial responses to the readings, as well as any questions they may have.
- Ask for volunteers to share some of their daily responses from this week from *The Bible Year* devotional.
- If you are using *The Bible Year* videos, play the video for today's session now.
- Continue your discussion of the week's Bible passages with the questions below.

Discussion Questions

1. Scholars generally believe Mark originally ended at verse 16:8. Why would the Resurrection frighten the women? How does such an ending connect to Mark's portrayal of Jesus's disciples throughout his Gospel (examples: 4:40; 6:51-52; 9:10, 29, 32)?
2. When, if ever, does fear keep you from saying anything about the risen Jesus—and how, if at all, do you overcome such fear?
3. Why is Luke writing his Gospel for Theophilus (1:1-4)? Have you ever helped another Christian understand what they have been taught about Jesus? How? How does your congregation educate its members in what they believe?
4. Both Zechariah and Mary react to Gabriel's announcements with questions (1:18, 34). Why is Mary's question welcomed and Zechariah's is not?

Do you think any questions to God are "off limits"? Why or why not?
5. Reread Mary's song of praise, the Magnificat (1:47-55). Find and listen to at least one musical setting of it. What does Mary tell us about God's values and priorities? How are they being seen in her experience? Where, if at all, do you find you and your congregation in Mary's song?
6. What is the political situation into which Jesus was born (2:1-3)? How are the angelic announcements of Jesus's birth political statements (2:10-14)? How does the Christmas story challenge political realities in today's world?
7. Matthew traced Jesus's genealogy back to Abraham; Luke traces it back to God (3:23-38). What significance, if any, do you find in this difference?
8. Luke's account of Jesus's temptations ends with an ominous note about the devil's timing (4:13). How do we learn to recognize times when evil can act, that we may resist it as God's people?

Closing

- Ask for several volunteers to summarize what they have found most meaningful about your discussion or about the biblical text this week. How might God be calling them to respond to it?
- Invite the group to raise any prayer concerns or lift up any reasons for joy and thanksgiving.
- Lead the group in a short closing prayer or invite a volunteer to do so.

Session 40

Luke 4:14–14:35

Overview

After Jesus preaches in his hometown of Nazareth, the people in the synagogue try to throw him off a cliff. Continuing his ministry of teaching and healing elsewhere, he calls disciples, including the fishermen Simon, James, and John, who catch a miraculous haul of fish when following Jesus's command.

Jesus declares God's blessings on those who are poor, who hunger, and who weep. Among other miracles, he feeds crowds of thousands with a few loaves and fish. Women from various social backgrounds follow Jesus.

Simon Peter confesses Jesus as Messiah, and Jesus talks of his own imminent suffering, death, and resurrection, teaching his disciples they must voluntarily suffer to follow him. Peter, James, and John see Jesus speaking in glory with Moses and Elijah on a mountain.

Jesus teaches in parables, including stories about a Samaritan who helps a man beaten and left for dead; a man who hoarded great wealth for himself, only to suddenly die; and a barren fig tree spared from destruction and given more time to bear fruit.

Opening

- Begin with prayer.

- Invite a volunteer or volunteers to summarize the week's readings, using the overview above as a reference.
- Invite the group to share initial responses to the readings, as well as any questions they may have.
- Ask for volunteers to share some of their daily responses from this week from *The Bible Year* devotional.
- If you are using *The Bible Year* videos, play the video for today's session now.
- Continue your discussion of the week's Bible passages with the questions below.

Discussion Questions

1. Why does Jesus say he fulfills the text from Isaiah (Luke 4:16-19; see Isaiah 58:6; 61:1-2)? How do the stories about Elijah and Elisha he alludes to (see 1 Kings 17; 2 Kings 5) illustrate that text?
2. Why does Jesus's sermon provoke such a violent response (Luke 4:28-30)? When, if ever, has a sermon made you angry, and why might we want to pay close attention if one does?
3. How does Simon react after the miraculous catch of fish (5:1-11)? Why? How, specifically and practically, do you and your congregation go about "catching people" for Jesus today? What might this miracle suggest about how to discern whether or not we are successful at it?
4. Compare Luke 6:20-26—the beginning of the "Sermon on the Plain" (6:17)—with the Beatitudes from the "Sermon on the Mount" in Matthew 5:1-12. How are they alike and different, and what do the differences suggest about Luke's view of Jesus? Do you prefer one version of these sayings over the other? Why or why not?
5. In the other Gospels, a woman anoints Jesus to prepare him for burial (Matthew 26:6-13; Mark 14:3-9; John 12:1-8). What motivates the woman to do so in Luke's

story (7:36-50)? How does the woman prove more hospitable to Jesus than Simon, his dinner host?
6. What is the most dramatic thing you have done, whether or not anyone else saw it, to express your love to God?
7. The parable of the "good Samaritan" is unique to Luke (10:25-37). Why do you think Jesus doesn't answer the lawyer's second question (v. 29) but instead tells him a story that poses a new question (v. 36)? In Jesus's day, many Jews would never have expected to find a "good" Samaritan, or vice versa. How can and does Jesus's story challenge prejudice in our day?

Closing

- Ask for several volunteers to summarize what they have found most meaningful about your discussion or about the biblical text this week. How might God be calling them to respond to it?
- Invite the group to raise any prayer concerns or lift up any reasons for joy and thanksgiving.
- Lead the group in a short closing prayer or invite a volunteer to do so.

SESSION 41

Luke 15:1–24:53

Overview

Jesus continues to tell parables, including: a triplet of tales about what is lost being found; a dishonest household manager; a rich man and the poor man he ignores; an unjust judge a widow bothers into doing his job; and a Pharisee and a tax collector.

Jesus heals ten men who have skin disease, only one of whom, a Samaritan, returns to give thanks. He visits the home of the tax collector Zacchaeus, small in stature but whose act of gratitude and repentance proves large.

He enters Jerusalem, weeping over the city's failure to recognize its visitation from God. He disputes with religious leaders who oppose him and foretells the Temple's destruction and the coming of "the Human One" in the messianic age.

Betrayed by Judas and denied by Peter, Jesus is crucified. One of the two criminals crucified alongside him mocks him, but the other asks Jesus to remember him in his kingdom. Jesus is buried, but the women who later go to his tomb to anoint his body find it unsealed, and two men tell them Jesus has been raised. That same day, Jesus appears to two disciples walking to Emmaus, and then to all his disciples. He blesses them and ascends to heaven.

Opening

- Begin with prayer.
- Invite a volunteer or volunteers to summarize the week's readings, using the overview above as a reference.
- Invite the group to share initial responses to the readings, as well as any questions they may have.
- Ask for volunteers to share some of their daily responses from this week from *The Bible Year* devotional.
- If you are using *The Bible Year* videos, play the video for today's session now.
- Continue your discussion of the week's Bible passages with the questions below.

Discussion Questions

1. What connections can you make among Jesus's three parables of what is lost being found (Luke 15:1-32)? How well do these stories fit the context Luke gives them (15:1-2), and why?

2. Which character in the parable about the lost son do you identify with most? What does this parable have to teach us about our relationship with God and one another?

3. How do (or how ought) Jesus's stories and sayings about money in Luke 16 instruct Jesus's followers today in the proper use of wealth? How do we avoid becoming slaves to wealth (16:13)?

4. Are there any "Lazaruses" at your or your congregation's "gate" (16:20)? If so, how are you caring for them? If not, to what gates would God have you go and find them?

5. Why do you think nine of the ten healed men did not return to thank Jesus (17:11-19)? Why do you think the Samaritan did? Did his return genuinely surprise

Jesus? Why or why not? What can this incident show us about God's relationship with those we consider "foreigners"?
6. First-century Jews often despised tax collectors as collaborators with the occupying Roman army, especially since many of the tax collectors kept much of the funds they collected for themselves. How do you imagine the crowd reacted to Jesus's interactions with Zacchaeus (19:1-10)?
7. Why do you think Jesus called to Zacchaeus? Do you think Zacchaeus followed through on his promise (19:8)? Why or why not?
8. How does Luke's "Easter story" (24:1-50) differ from Matthew's and Mark's? Why do the disciples going to Emmaus fail to recognize the risen Jesus, and what happens so that they do (24:13-32)? Have you ever realized, after the fact, you were in the presence of the risen Jesus? What happened?

Closing

- Ask for several volunteers to summarize what they have found most meaningful about your discussion or about the biblical text this week. How might God be calling them to respond to it?
- Invite the group to raise any prayer concerns or lift up any reasons for joy and thanksgiving.
- Lead the group in a short closing prayer or invite a volunteer to do so.

SESSION 42

John 1:1–10:42

Overview

John starts his story of Jesus at the beginning of all things, when God created through the Word, God's only Son, who became flesh in Jesus.

John the Baptist testifies to Jesus. Some of John's disciples follow him, and they call others. Attending a wedding in Cana with his disciples, Jesus turns six large jars' worth of water into wine.

In Jerusalem to celebrate Passover, Jesus drives out the moneychangers and speaks of his death. He tells Nicodemus, a Pharisee, that none can see God's kingdom without being "born anew" (3:3).

Leaving Judea, Jesus travels through Samaria, where he meets a woman who testifies about him to her village. Over the next year, Jesus performs miraculous healings and feedings, and speaks of his authority as the Son of God who does his Father's will. His teachings about eating his flesh and drinking his blood are so difficult that many followers leave, but Simon and others remain.

While Jesus is in Jerusalem again for the Festival of Booths, Pharisees send Temple police to arrest him. They do not, so impressed are they by his teaching. Jesus debates with the leaders, denouncing them as demonic. His healing of a man born blind only exacerbates his conflict with them.

John 1:1–10:42

Opening

- Begin with prayer.
- Invite a volunteer or volunteers to summarize the week's readings, using the overview above as a reference.
- Invite the group to share initial responses to the readings, as well as any questions they may have.
- Ask for volunteers to share some of their daily responses from this week from *The Bible Year* devotional.
- If you are using *The Bible Year* videos, play the video for today's session now.
- Continue your discussion of the week's Bible passages with the questions below.

Discussion Questions

1. Giving true testimony about Jesus is an important theme in John's Gospel. What specific claims about Jesus's identity and purpose do you find in this week's chapters? Which of these mean the most to you?
2. In the Fourth Gospel, unlike the first three, John the Baptist seems to have no independent message, but baptizes solely to point toward Jesus (1:19-34; 3:22-30). Might God be calling you or your congregation to "decrease" in some ways that Jesus may "increase"? How?
3. Jesus turns a great amount of water into wine as his first "sign" (2:1-11). What does this miracle signify? How is it about more than making sure a wedding party can go on?
4. References to Jesus's "hour" or "time" occur frequently in John (2:4; 4:21-23; 5:25-28; 7:6-8, 30; 8:20). When is Jesus's hour, and what is its importance?
5. People in John frequently misunderstand what Jesus says. As you read this week's chapters, who did you notice misunderstanding Jesus, and how did they?

How do some misunderstandings differ from others? Which of them, if any, do you empathize with?
6. When, like Simon, have you confessed both your misunderstanding of and faith in Jesus (6:68-69)?
7. Christians today must confront John's relentless and nearly completely negative depiction of "the Jews" (in this week's readings see especially 8:22-59; 10:22-39), which has helped fuel centuries of hatred toward Jews. Given Jesus and his earliest disciples were Jews, how ought we understand "the Jews" in John?
8. Jesus provokes much division throughout John's Gospel. How does Jesus divide people today? How do we discern which of these divisions, if any, are legitimate, and which are actually failings of the church we should seek to overcome?

Closing

+ Ask for several volunteers to summarize what they have found most meaningful about your discussion or about the biblical text this week. How might God be calling them to respond to it?
+ Invite the group to raise any prayer concerns or lift up any reasons for joy and thanksgiving.
+ Lead the group in a short closing prayer or invite a volunteer to do so.

SESSION 43

John 11:1– Acts 5:16

Overview

After Jesus raises his friend Lazarus from death, the high priest Caiaphas and Pharisees who oppose Jesus plot Jesus's death.

Jesus comes to Jerusalem to celebrate Passover. As they dine before Passover, Jesus washes his disciples' feet. He teaches them they must serve and love each other as he has served and loved them. He promises to send the Holy Spirit and prays for their unity and witness to him.

Jesus presents himself to Judas and the soldiers who come to arrest him in a garden. As Caiaphas interrogates Jesus, Peter denies knowing him. Tried and sentenced to death by Pilate, Jesus is crucified.

Mary Magdalene sees the risen Jesus at his tomb on the first day of the week. He appears to his disciples that night—and again a week later, when Thomas is present to see Jesus's wounds. Jesus also appears to some disciples as they fish, causing a miraculous catch and charging Peter to care for his "sheep."

The Acts of the Apostles was written by the author of Luke. In its opening chapters, Luke writes of Jesus's ascension; the coming of the Holy Spirit to Jesus's followers on Pentecost; the preaching of Peter and the apostles about Jesus, and the miracles they perform; and the communal life the church shares.

Opening

- Begin with prayer.
- Invite a volunteer or volunteers to summarize the week's readings, using the overview above as a reference.
- Invite the group to share initial responses to the readings, as well as any questions they may have.
- Ask for volunteers to share some of their daily responses from this week from *The Bible Year* devotional.
- If you are using *The Bible Year* videos, play the video for today's session now.
- Continue your discussion of the week's Bible passages with the questions below.

Discussion Questions

1. Jesus's raising of Lazarus is the last miraculous "sign" he performs in John (11:1-44). What does it signify? How does it address Martha's "misunderstanding" with Jesus (vv. 23-27)?
2. Why does Jesus cry before raising Lazarus (vv. 35-37)? Why is Lazarus still in danger after Jesus raises him (12:9-11)? Does being associated with Jesus and the new life he gives put you at risk? Why or why not?
3. How does John's account of Jesus's last meal with his disciples differ from those of the other Gospels (13:1-38)? Why does Jesus command his followers to wash one another's feet? What practices might approximate the significance of a household servant washing a visitor's feet today?
4. What specifically does Jesus tell his disciples about the Holy Spirit (14:15-17, 25-26; 15:26-27; 16:7-15)? When and how have you and your congregation experienced the Spirit's work, as Jesus describes it?

5. How does Jesus identify himself for Mary Magdalene (20:14-16) and for his disciples (20:19-21, 26-28) after he is raised? How do you and your congregation recognize the risen Jesus in your lives and in the world?
6. On Pentecost, the Holy Spirit empowers the church to speak the gospel in ways the world can hear. What "languages" (literal or otherwise) does the church need to speak today to communicate the good news of salvation? How do we pray for the Spirit to help us?
7. Even if Luke paints an idealized portrait of early church life (Acts 2:43-47; 4:32-37), how much of the fellowship he describes would he find in your congregation? How much should today's church strive to be like the early church, and why?

Closing

+ Ask for several volunteers to summarize what they have found most meaningful about your discussion or about the biblical text this week. How might God be calling them to respond to it?
+ Invite the group to raise any prayer concerns or lift up any reasons for joy and thanksgiving.
+ Lead the group in a short closing prayer or invite a volunteer to do so.

Session 44

Acts 5:17–23:35

Overview

As the church grows, it is persecuted. The Jewish high priest and council arrest and try Stephen, a prominent church leader. When Stephen accuses them of resisting the Holy Spirit, they stone him to death. Saul (also called Paul, see Acts 13:9) goes to Damascus to arrest Jesus's followers. But on his way there, the risen Jesus suddenly appears to him, and he is blinded. After Ananias, a disciple, heals him, Saul begins to preach that Jesus is the Messiah.

On a journey of his own, Peter also has a vision from God, which convinces him to baptize the Gentile centurion Cornelius and his household after the Holy Spirit empowers them to speak in other languages as Peter is preaching to them.

When questions about whether Gentiles who believe in Jesus must obey the Torah come to a head, the church's leaders meet at a council in Jerusalem to debate the issue. The council decides Gentiles must only observe the Law's prohibitions against ritually impure food and against fornication.

Paul undertakes several missionary journeys to Gentile cities, proclaiming the gospel. While he is back in Jerusalem, opponents accuse him of teaching Jews to violate the Law. Tried before Roman and Jewish authorities, Paul is sent for a hearing before the Roman governor Felix.

Opening

- Begin with prayer.
- Invite a volunteer or volunteers to summarize the week's readings, using the overview above as a reference.
- Invite the group to share initial responses to the readings, as well as any questions they may have.
- Ask for volunteers to share some of their daily responses from this week from *The Bible Year* devotional.
- If you are using *The Bible Year* videos, play the video for today's session now.
- Continue your discussion of the week's Bible passages with the questions below.

Discussion Questions

1. How is Stephen's arrest, trial, and death both like and unlike that of Jesus (6:8–7:60)? What do you think the similarities indicate? What is the point Stephen wants to make with his summary of Israel's history with God? What does he include and exclude in order to make it?
2. Where do Christians today risk martyrdom for their faith? What do you and your congregation do to support them?
3. How does Philip's encounter with the Ethiopian official (8:26-39) demonstrate the gospel's ability to speak to people outside the religious community's usual boundaries? How do or could you help others "understand what [they] are reading" (v. 30) so they can hear God addressing them personally through Scripture?
4. The conversion of Saul (Paul) is the most dramatic in Acts, but what "conversion" does Ananias undergo in Acts 9? How does Peter undergo a "conversion" in Acts 10? To which of these conversion experiences, if any, can you most relate?

The Bible Year: Leader Guide

5. In what ways is conversion a one-time experience for Christians, and in what ways is it ongoing?
6. The Jerusalem church council intended its decision (15:22-29) to preserve fellowship between Jewish and Gentile believers in Jesus,[8] but for most of Acts we watch Christianity becoming a Gentile faith. How does Luke see this development fulfilling ancient Scripture (15:13-18)? How ought our shared "family history" shape relationships between Jews and Christians today?
7. Which of the many stories of Paul's missionary journeys in this week's chapters most interests or intrigues you? Why? Do you or your congregation support missionaries today? Where and how?

Closing

- Ask for several volunteers to summarize what they have found most meaningful about your discussion or about the biblical text this week. How might God be calling them to respond to it?
- Invite the group to raise any prayer concerns or lift up any reasons for joy and thanksgiving.
- Lead the group in a short closing prayer or invite a volunteer to do so.

SESSION 45

Acts 24:1– Romans 13:14

Overview

After defending his faith before Felix, Paul spends two years in custody. When Festus succeeds Felix as governor, Paul wants to be heard before the emperor. Felix has Paul defend himself before Herod Agrippa, ruler of Judea. Agrippa is not moved by Paul's appeal for him to believe in Jesus, but he does think Paul could have been freed had he not appealed to Rome.

Sailing with other prisoners to Rome, Paul and the ship's crew are shipwrecked on the island of Malta in a storm. Paul heals many people there, and even miraculously survives a snakebite. Once in Rome, Paul spends two years under house arrest waiting for his trial. All the while, he preaches the gospel.

In his letter to Christians in Rome, Paul argues that while all people, Gentile and Jew, have sinned, God justifies all by grace through Jesus's atoning death. All who are baptized into Jesus share his death and his risen life, and must be slaves of righteousness rather than sin. The Law, God's holy and good gift, became an occasion for sin to condemn us; but Jesus has condemned sin. Paul believes God has, for the time being, caused Israel to stumble so that Gentiles may also be saved.

Opening

- Begin with prayer.
- Invite a volunteer or volunteers to summarize the week's readings, using the overview above as a reference.
- Invite the group to share initial responses to the readings, as well as any questions they may have.
- Ask for volunteers to share some of their daily responses from this week from *The Bible Year* devotional.
- If you are using *The Bible Year* videos, play the video for today's session now.
- Continue your discussion of the week's Bible passages with the questions below.

Discussion Questions

1. Why do you think Luke ended Acts without recounting Paul's trial in Rome, which readers are led to expect from verse 25:10 on? How does the Book of Acts as a whole show Jesus's followers fulfilling his words in verse 1:8?
2. How are you and your congregation involved today in proclaiming the gospel both locally and "to the ends of the earth"?
3. In Romans 1–2, Paul recites what would have been familiar claims of Gentile sinfulness before accusing his Jewish readers of sin. When are you most tempted to pass judgment on others? How do you handle this temptation?
4. Does avoiding judging others mean accepting all behavior as permissible? Why or why not?
5. What does Paul mean by "faith" in Romans? Where does faith come from? How does Abraham's story illustrate faith (chapter 4)? What is the outcome of faith (5:1-11)?
6. For Paul, sin is more than a "bad deed"—sin is a cosmic power actively exploiting God's good gifts, such as the

Law (3:20; 5:13; 7:7-13). What other good gifts from God do you believe sin exploits? Why? How does Jesus save us from sin? How do we relate to God's good gifts, including the Law, as Christians?

7. Though he is perplexed and grieved over his fellow Jews' rejection of Jesus (chapters 9–11), Paul concludes "all Israel will be saved" (11:26). What does his teaching mean for claims that the church somehow "replaced" Israel as God's chosen people? What does Paul himself say to such claims (11:17-24)?

8. What gives Paul his confidence that nothing can separate us from God's love in Jesus (8:31-39)? When are you most and least likely to share his confidence? With whom could you and your congregation share this promise this week?

Closing

- Ask for several volunteers to summarize what they have found most meaningful about your discussion or about the biblical text this week. How might God be calling them to respond to it?
- Invite the group to raise any prayer concerns or lift up any reasons for joy and thanksgiving.
- Lead the group in a short closing prayer or invite a volunteer to do so.

SESSION 46

Romans 14:1– 2 Corinthians 3:18

Overview

Paul concludes his letter to Rome by urging the believers to encourage one another in faith and to seek each other's good over their own. He tells them of his intent to visit after he delivers an offering he has collected for the church in Jerusalem.

Paul's correspondence with Christians in Corinth is less polished and often confrontational. He organized this congregation and is upset to hear of their divisions and, he believes, departures from the gospel he preached.

In 1 Corinthians, Paul instructs the Corinthians about sexual morality, the inappropriateness of taking each other to court, whether to marry or be celibate in light of Jesus's imminent coming, whether believers may eat meat sacrificed to idols, how to properly celebrate the Lord's Supper, about spiritual gifts, and about the resurrection of the dead. He stresses that God's wisdom and power do not look like what the world calls "wisdom" or "power," and urges his readers at every turn to love each other and glorify God in their conduct.

Paul begins 2 Corinthians explaining his failure to visit as he had planned, and by claiming the Corinthians themselves are the only defense of his ministry he requires.

Opening

- Begin with prayer.
- Invite a volunteer or volunteers to summarize the week's readings, using the overview above as a reference.
- Invite the group to share initial responses to the readings, as well as any questions they may have.
- Ask for volunteers to share some of their daily responses from this week from *The Bible Year* devotional.
- If you are using *The Bible Year* videos, play the video for today's session now.
- Continue your discussion of the week's Bible passages with the questions below.

Discussion Questions

1. What appears to be the reason the Corinthians have divided themselves into factions, and how does Paul address this problem (1 Corinthians 1:10-16; 3:5-10; 4:6-7)?
2. When has your congregation been divided, or is it divided now, into opposing camps? Over what issue(s)? How did or how might Paul's words to the Corinthians offer your congregation ways forward?
3. Why would Paul's preaching of "Christ crucified" be a "scandal" and "foolishness" to some (1:23)? What is Paul's response (1:25-29)? When have you or your congregation witnessed the wisdom of God's foolishness and the power of God's strength for yourselves?
4. How do we keep ourselves aligned with God's definition of wisdom and strength, over and against the many alternate definitions we encounter in the world?

5. Paul believes the kingdom of God's arrival in the world is imminent (7:29-31). How does this perspective shape his advice to the Corinthians throughout 1 Corinthians? Can Christians share Paul's perspective some two thousand years later? If so, how?
6. What difference do scriptural promises of Jesus's coming and God's final intervention in history, such as those in 1 Corinthians 15, make for how we live today?
7. Why does Paul argue some of the Corinthians should refrain from eating meat that had been sacrificed to idols, which they later bought in the marketplaces (8:1-13)? When was a time you have restrained your own exercise of freedom for someone else's good?
8. What is wrong about the way the Corinthians are celebrating the Lord's Supper (11:17-34)? Does your congregation see gaps between more and less affluent members? If so, what are you doing to address them? How is your congregation "without correctly understanding the body" of Christ (11:29; 12:27) before it celebrates the Lord's Supper (Communion or Eucharist)?

Closing

- Ask for several volunteers to summarize what they have found most meaningful about your discussion or about the biblical text this week. How might God be calling them to respond to it?
- Invite the group to raise any prayer concerns or lift up any reasons for joy and thanksgiving.
- Lead the group in a short closing prayer or invite a volunteer to do so.

SESSION 47

2 Corinthians 4:1– Ephesians 2:22

Overview

As 2 Corinthians continues, Paul explains his ministry as one through which people are reconciled to God. It becomes apparent that Paul and the Corinthians also need to be reconciled to each other. Paul has previously grieved them and must assure them of his ongoing affection as he appeals to them to contribute to his collection for the church in Jerusalem. But he also vehemently defends his ministry's integrity against apparent disparaging from self-proclaimed "super-apostles" (12:11). Paul's conduct and his visions, but especially his sufferings, confirm him as an authentic messenger for Christ.

Competition from those who preach another gospel is also a major theme in Paul's letter to believers in Galatia. The Galatian Christians are turning to those who tell them that Gentiles who believe in Jesus as Messiah must obey the commandments in Torah, including male circumcision. Against this position, Paul insists God saves both Jews and Gentiles by grace. Faith removes believers from the Law's obligations and unites Jew and Gentile in Christ. He urges his readers to live in this freedom, cultivating the Spirit's fruits in their lives.

The Bible Year: Leader Guide

Paul's letter to Christians in Ephesus begins by praising God for revealing God's plan to unite all things in Christ, and for making Jews and Gentiles into "one new person" (Ephesians 2:15) in him.

Opening

- Begin with prayer.
- Invite a volunteer or volunteers to summarize the week's readings, using the overview above as a reference.
- Invite the group to share initial responses to the readings, as well as any questions they may have.
- Ask for volunteers to share some of their daily responses from this week from *The Bible Year* devotional.
- If you are using *The Bible Year* videos, play the video for today's session now.
- Continue your discussion of the week's Bible passages with the questions below.

Discussion Questions

1. Why does God use frail humans whose bodies are "breaking down" (2 Corinthians 4:16), mere "clay pots" (4:7), to accomplish the divine ministry of reconciling the world (4:1–5:21)?
2. Who have been the "ambassadors who represent Christ" (5:20) in your life who have been important in your relationship to God?
3. What does Christian generosity look like, and what motivates it, according to Paul (8:1–9:15)? How much or how little does your congregation talk about using money as Paul does, and why? When and to what or whom do you give your money most "cheerfully," and why?
4. How does Paul defend his claim to be "an apostle" (12:12) in 2 Corinthians 10–12? What is at stake in his argument with the so-called "super-apostles"?

What criteria do and should Christians use to discern who is truly leading them in Christ's ways?
5. Why did Paul oppose Cephas (Peter) at Antioch (Galatians 2:11-21)? Were Peter asked to present his side in their argument, what do you imagine he would say?
6. Why does Paul—himself a circumcised, devout and observant Jew—that "being circumcised or not being circumcised doesn't matter" (5:6)?
7. How can we tell if we are elevating adherence to rules over reliance on grace in our faith?
8. What are the "fruits" of a life lived by God's Spirit (5:16-26)? Where do you see these fruits in the life of your congregation? How do others see these fruits in you?

Closing

+ Ask for several volunteers to summarize what they have found most meaningful about your discussion or about the biblical text this week. How might God be calling them to respond to it?
+ Invite the group to raise any prayer concerns or lift up any reasons for joy and thanksgiving.
+ Lead the group in a short closing prayer or invite a volunteer to do so.

SESSION 48

Ephesians 3:1– 1 Thessalonians 3:13

Overview

In Ephesians, Paul prays for his readers, urges their unity, and describes the new quality of life to which Christ has called them, including codes of conduct for Christian households.

Paul's letter to Christians in Philippi echoes with the joy Paul feels in his faith and for his readers, even though he is imprisoned. He calls on readers to imitate Christ's own humility in their relationships with one another and exults in the righteousness God freely gives in Jesus Christ.

In the Letter to the Colossians, Paul stresses Jesus Christ's supremacy over all other earthly or heavenly powers. He warns readers against relying on anything—law, ritual, mystic experiences—other than Christ. He exhorts them to a new quality of life and sketches a code of conduct for Christian households.

In his first letter to the church in Thessalonica, Paul recalls how he worked his trade to relieve the believers from financially supporting him as he preached. He also recounts sending his co-missionary Timothy to encourage them when he was unable to be with them himself. Paul is thankful for Timothy's good report about the Thessalonians and expresses his eagerness to be with them again.

Ephesians 3:1–1 Thessalonians 3:13

Opening

- Begin with prayer.
- Invite a volunteer or volunteers to summarize the week's readings, using the overview above as a reference.
- Invite the group to share initial responses to the readings, as well as any questions they may have.
- Ask for volunteers to share some of their daily responses from this week from *The Bible Year* devotional.
- If you are using *The Bible Year* videos, play the video for today's session now.
- Continue your discussion of the week's Bible passages with the questions below.

Discussion Questions

1. The letters to the Ephesians (5:21–6:9) and Colossians (3:18–4:1) include "household codes," or lists of duties household members owe each other, a form borrowed from Greek and Roman philosophers.[9] What do the codes prescribe for husbands and wives? for parents and children? for masters and slaves? How relevant do you think these codes are or should be for Christian households today, and why?
2. Ephesians 6:10-17 describes "the full armor of God." How do we wear this "armor"? Which of its pieces do you find yourself relying on most? Which could you stand to use more often?
3. Where do you see evidence of the spiritual struggle Paul describes in Ephesians 6:10-17? How does—or how ought—remembering our true enemies aren't "human enemies" (6:12) shape the way we relate to other people with whom we are in conflict?
4. How did Jesus Christ demonstrate humility according to Philippians 2:1-11? How does Paul want his readers

The Bible Year: Leader Guide

to demonstrate humility? What distinguishes true, Christian humility from false humility (or just being modest)?

5. Who is the humblest follower of Christ you have personally known, and how does their witness influence you?
6. Paul lists quite the resume in Philippians 3:4b-6, but regards it all as "sewer trash" (v. 8, or "rubbish," in some translations)[10] compared to "knowing Christ." What in your background and your achievements are you proudest of, even justly so? How easily could you (or have you) dismissed those things as worthless next to the call of Christ?
7. How would you answer someone who said, "Christians worship a God who doesn't want anyone to feel good about themselves or what they do"?
8. How does Paul emphasize Jesus's superiority in Colossians (1:15-23; 2:9-10)? Why might Paul have thought it necessary to stress Jesus's supreme nature (2:8-19; 3:1-4)? What competes with Jesus for supremacy in your life? in your congregation's?

Closing

+ Ask for several volunteers to summarize what they have found most meaningful about your discussion or about the biblical text this week. How might God be calling them to respond to it?
+ Invite the group to raise any prayer concerns or lift up any reasons for joy and thanksgiving.
+ Lead the group in a short closing prayer or invite a volunteer to do so.

SESSION 49

1 Thessalonians 4:1– Titus 3:15

Overview

Paul encourages the Thessalonians with his teaching that those among them who have died will be raised when Jesus comes from heaven, and then all, dead or alive, will be with Jesus forever. That day will come suddenly, and believers must stay watchful and faithful.

The second Letter to the Thessalonians speaks of Jesus's coming in a different way: it will mean fiery wrath and eternal punishment for those who disobey the gospel. That day will not arrive until a "person who is lawless" (2:3) emerges and declares himself God. Until then, believers must work quietly and diligently to earn their living and must not tire of doing what is right.

In two letters to his protégé, Timothy, Paul instructs the young man in how to faithfully minister to God's people. Paul encourages Timothy to hold on to the faith in the midst of troubled times to come and looks forward to "the champion's wreath" he will receive from Jesus (2 Timothy 4:8).

Paul's letter to Titus urges its recipient to teach correct doctrine, proper Christian household conduct, and to exhort believers to mutual love and good works in gratitude for God's saving mercy.

Opening

- Begin with prayer.
- Invite a volunteer or volunteers to summarize the week's readings, using the overview above as a reference.
- Invite the group to share initial responses to the readings, as well as any questions they may have.
- Ask for volunteers to share some of their daily responses from this week from *The Bible Year* devotional.
- If you are using *The Bible Year* videos, play the video for today's session now.
- Continue your discussion of the week's Bible passages with the questions below.

Discussion Questions

1. How does Paul seek to answer his readers' apparent questions about Jesus's delay in coming (1 Thessalonians 4:13–5:11)? Was Paul mistaken about "a message from the Lord" (4:15) he tells his readers? Why or why not?
2. What do you imagine Paul might say to modern Christians about Jesus's return? Why?
3. How are 1 Thessalonians 4:13–5:11 and 2 Thessalonians 1:5–2:12 alike and different in their descriptions of and attitudes toward the day of the Lord? Do you find these visions of that day contradictory or complementary? Why? How do they shape the way you live today?
4. What criteria for church leaders does 1 Timothy specify (especially in 3:1-13 and 4:6-16; compare Titus 1:5-9)? Which of these criteria, if any, does your congregation or denomination recognize, and which ones does it not? What additional criteria do you use?
5. How do you determine whether church leaders "lead well" (1 Timothy 5:17)? How much value should churches today place on formal leadership roles? Why?

6. In 2 Timothy 4:6-8, Paul takes stock of his life spent faithfully serving Christ. Why does he compare such a life to athletic competition? As you look back over your life to this point, however long you have lived, how do you assess how well you have been "competing" for Christ?

7. Paul discusses some purposes of Scripture (by which he meant the writings Christians call the Old Testament) in 2 Timothy 3:16-17. How have you seen Scripture fulfill these purposes for yourself? What else do you believe Scripture is and does, and why?

Closing

- Ask for several volunteers to summarize what they have found most meaningful about your discussion or about the biblical text this week. How might God be calling them to respond to it?
- Invite the group to raise any prayer concerns or lift up any reasons for joy and thanksgiving.
- Lead the group in a short closing prayer or invite a volunteer to do so.

SESSION 50

Philemon–James 2:26

Overview

From prison, Paul writes his friend Philemon, urging him to welcome Paul's emissary Onesimus—from whom Philemon has been estranged for some unspecified reason—as he would welcome Paul himself.

The letter to the Hebrews urges its readers to remain faithful despite rejection from their neighbors and persecution. The author draws on Scripture and Temple ritual to argue Jesus is superior to God's angelic messengers because Jesus is God's Son and believers' sympathetic high priest. Like the ancient high priest Melchizedek, Jesus is an eternal priest. Jesus offered himself as the ultimate sacrifice to deal with sin, yet lives forever to intercede for sinners, and through him God has established a new covenant of salvation. The author reminds readers of God's faithful people who have preceded them, urging them also to persevere until the day of the Lord rather than spurn God's grace.

In his letter, the apostle James warns his readers to stop showing favoritism to the wealthy in their gatherings and to instead meet the basic needs of those who are poor and vulnerable. James cites Abraham and Rahab as examples of people who were justified with God by their works, for "faith without actions has no value at all" (2:20).

Opening

- Begin with prayer.
- Invite a volunteer or volunteers to summarize the week's readings, using the overview above as a reference.
- Invite the group to share initial responses to the readings, as well as any questions they may have.
- Ask for volunteers to share some of their daily responses from this week from *The Bible Year* devotional.
- If you are using *The Bible Year* videos, play the video for today's session now.
- Continue your discussion of the week's Bible passages with the questions below.

Discussion Questions

1. Centuries of Christian readers have assumed Onesimus was Philemon's slave, but in verse 16 Paul urges Philemon to welcome Onesimus "no longer as a slave but more than a slave," which may not indicate their actual relationship.[11] How does assuming Onesimus was or wasn't Philemon's slave affect the letter's meaning?
2. What does Paul promise to do to help Philemon and Onesimus reconcile as brothers in Christ? Whose debts would you repay (or have you repaid) to help reconciliation happen?
3. What are the urgent stakes the author of Hebrews believes he is addressing (2:1-4; 3:12-14; 6:4-12; 10:26-31)? Have you ever encouraged someone who was wavering in their faith to persevere? Have you ever needed such encouragement yourself? What happened?
4. Do you believe true faith can be lost—and if lost, regained? Why or why not?

5. How does Hebrews say Jesus is superior to angels (1:1-14)? to Moses (3:1-6)? to the priests of Israel (7:15-28; 9:23–10:18)? Does regarding God's covenant with Israel as "old and outdated" (8:13) contradict other New Testament teachings (examples: Matthew 5:17-20; Romans 11:25-32)? How does such a view pose dangers to Jews today?
6. How can and do modern Christians affirm faith in Jesus without putting him at odds with his own Jewish heritage?
7. Which, if any, of the examples of faith in Hebrews 11 do you personally find most inspiring and encouraging, and why? Who are the people you have personally known whom you count among the "great cloud of witnesses" (12:1) cheering you on as you, as they did, follow Jesus?
8. How does James conclude Abraham and Rahab were justified by works (2:14-26) while Paul concluded Abraham was justified by faith (Romans 4:1-12)? Do these two readings of Abraham's story contradict each other? Why or why not?

Closing

+ Ask for several volunteers to summarize what they have found most meaningful about your discussion or about the biblical text this week. How might God be calling them to respond to it?
+ Invite the group to raise any prayer concerns or lift up any reasons for joy and thanksgiving.
+ Lead the group in a short closing prayer or invite a volunteer to do so.

SESSION 51

James 3:1– 1 John 5:21

Overview

James warns his readers that those who teach the faith will be held strictly accountable and urges them to humble themselves before God and one another. He cautions them to avoid making arrogant plans and making oaths, denounces those who are rich and defraud laborers, and commends prayer and anointing with oil for those who are sick.

The apostle Peter's first letter calls on Christians living among nonbelievers to accept suffering as a consequence of doing right, even as Christ did. Peter interprets his readers' suffering as a sign that God's judgment of the world is beginning with the faithful.

Peter's second letter urges readers to confirm their calling by righteous living. He warns them of false prophets who are doomed for destruction on the day of the Lord. That day seems slow to arrive, but Peter urges readers to regard its delay as proof of God's patient desire for all to repent.

The apostle John's first letter lifts up mutual love as the hallmark of Christian community. Because God loved us by sending Jesus as the atoning sacrifice for sin, Jesus's followers must love one another, in word and in deed.

Opening

- Begin with prayer.
- Invite a volunteer or volunteers to summarize the week's readings, using the overview above as a reference.
- Invite the group to share initial responses to the readings, as well as any questions they may have.
- Ask for volunteers to share some of their daily responses from this week from *The Bible Year* devotional.
- If you are using *The Bible Year* videos, play the video for today's session now.
- Continue your discussion of the week's Bible passages with the questions below.

Discussion Questions

1. How does James distinguish between worldly and heavenly wisdom, not only in verses 3:13-18 but also throughout his letter? Which of the issues James addresses do you find most pressing for you personally? for your congregation?
2. Both James (5:7-11) and Peter (1 Peter 2:18-25; 3:13-18a) counsel Christians to patiently endure suffering, but for different reasons. Describe each author's teaching on the subject. When are you patient in suffering? When are you not?
3. How differently, if at all, should Christians respond to their own unjust suffering and other people's unjust suffering? When, if ever, does faith in Christ demand resisting our own or others' unjust suffering?
4. James believes righteous people's prayers are "powerful in what it can achieve" (5:16), especially prayers for those who are sick (5:14-15). How do you and your congregation pray for those who are ill? What do you believe about the power of prayer—for those who are sick, and in other circumstances?

5. Who are "antichrists," according to John (1 John 2:18-25; 4:1-6)? What does this warning suggest about the situation John was addressing? How, if at all, does it relate to Christian communities today?
6. What are the consequences of Christians denying Jesus came "as a human" (1 John 4:2)? Does John's warning apply to those who hold a different faith, or no faith at all? Why or why not?
7. What is the relationship between loving God and loving one's fellow believers in 1 John (2:10-11; 3:14-18; 4:7-21)? What, specifically, does "love" look like for John? What does love look like in your congregation?
8. The letters of Peter and John devote significant attention to discerning true faith and true believers from false. How important is this task for churches today, and how can churches pursue it in Christlike ways?

Closing

- Ask for several volunteers to summarize what they have found most meaningful about your discussion or about the biblical text this week. How might God be calling them to respond to it?
- Invite the group to raise any prayer concerns or lift up any reasons for joy and thanksgiving.
- Lead the group in a short closing prayer or invite a volunteer to do so.

SESSION 52

2 John– Revelation 11:19

Overview

In 2 John, the author ("the elder") reminds believers to love each other and beware false teaching. In 3 John, the elder praises one Gaius for his faithfulness and hospitality—in contrast to one inhospitable Diotrephes, who goes so far as to expel believers who wish to welcome others.

In his letter, Jude urges readers to defend the faith against false teachers (described in much the same terms as the false prophets in 2 Peter). He reminds them the apostles predicted unbelievers and divisions, and calls on readers to strengthen themselves, entrusting them to God's care.

Revelation is an account of an apocalyptic vision of the risen Christ. The seer John, in an ecstatic vision on the island of Patmos, sees Christ, who gives him messages commending and chastising seven congregations across Asia Minor, calling them all to renewed faithfulness.

John is called up to heaven, where he sees a majestic vision of God's heavenly throne room. A Lamb who has been slaughtered yet lives opens a seven-sealed scroll, initiating a series of disasters on the earth. Seven angels blow trumpets, with similar results. Yet 144,000 people from

2 John–Revelation 11:19

Israel's tribes are sealed for salvation, and an innumerable multitude of martyrs from every nation are praising God and the Lamb in heaven.

Opening

- Begin with prayer.
- Invite a volunteer or volunteers to summarize the week's readings, using the overview above as a reference.
- Invite the group to share initial responses to the readings, as well as any questions they may have.
- Ask for volunteers to share some of their daily responses from this week from *The Bible Year* devotional.
- If you are using *The Bible Year* videos, play the video for today's session now.
- Continue your discussion of the week's Bible passages with the questions below.

Discussion Questions

1. In Revelation, John is given an otherwise inaccessible heavenly perspective. How would his vision of the risen Jesus encourage churches beginning to experience widespread persecution (1:9-20)? his vision of the occupied heavenly throne room (4:1-11)? his vision of the martyrs (7:9-17)?
2. What do poetic images like those John uses convey that more direct, "teaching" language cannot? What thoughts and feelings do these images spark in you?
3. Which of the seven churches does the risen Christ praise in Revelation 2–3, and why? Which does he find fault with, and why? How does he expose the way these churches see themselves, for better *and* for worse? Where—again, for better *and* for worse—do you recognize your congregation in these letters?
4. John is told "the Lion of the tribe of Judah" has conquered, but sees instead "a Lamb, standing

as if it had been slain" (5:1-7). What does this vision communicate about Jesus, and about God's understanding of power and victory?
5. How does John's vision in 7:1-10 of the sealed from Israel's twelve tribes (12,000 twelve times over, suggesting completion) as well as the uncountable throng "from every nation, tribe, people, and language" (7:9) expand our view of among whom God is active and who belongs to God? What practical implications does it have for the church's worship and work on earth today?
6. Depending on your Scripture translation, you may recognize Handel's "Hallelujah Chorus" in Revelations 11:15. What does affirming the coming of God's kingdom mean for the way we relate to the kingdoms of this world? How does it shape our involvement as citizens in a democratic "kingdom," with rights and responsibilities our first-century forebears could never have imagined?

Closing

- Ask for several volunteers to summarize what they have found most meaningful about your discussion or about the biblical text this week. How might God be calling them to respond to it?
- Invite the group to raise any prayer concerns or lift up any reasons for joy and thanksgiving.
- Lead the group in a short closing prayer or invite a volunteer to do so.

SESSION 53

Revelation 12:1–22:21

Overview

In the final section of Revelation, John sees a dragon in heaven threaten a woman giving birth. The son who is born is taken to God, and the woman escapes to God's care. Michael and his angels defeat the dragon, Satan, throwing him to earth where he persecutes Jesus's followers.

Two other beasts rise from the sea to worship the dragon and impose their authority on the earth's inhabitants. Seven angels pour bowls of God's wrath on the earth. Another angel announces the doom of Babylon, at which God's saints in heaven rejoice. The Word of God leads heaven's armies against the beasts, who are thrown into a lake of fire.

An angel imprisons Satan in a bottomless pit for a thousand years. Faithful martyrs are raised and rule with Christ. After the thousand years, Satan is released; he deceives the nations but is thrown into the lake of fire. The dead are judged according to their works; those whose names aren't in the book of life are thrown into the lake of fire, as are Death and Hades.

God creates a new heaven and a new earth, where God dwells in the midst of humanity forever. After describing the New Jerusalem, John closes with a fervent prayer for Christ's coming.

Opening

- Begin with prayer.
- Invite a volunteer or volunteers to summarize the week's readings, using the overview above as a reference.
- Invite the group to share initial responses to the readings, as well as any questions they may have.
- Ask for volunteers to share some of their daily responses from this week from *The Bible Year* devotional.
- If you are using *The Bible Year* videos, play the video for today's session now.
- Continue your discussion of the week's Bible passages with the questions below.

Discussion Questions

1. If the first half of Revelation is challenging for modern Christians to read (and it is), the second half, full of bizarre beasts, mystic numbers, and cryptic asides, is arguably even more so. Rather than starting with what is strange, focus first on what you found clear about these chapters. Which statements about God and Jesus grabbed your attention? Which images were vivid enough to evoke a strong emotional reaction?
2. How would you summarize John's message throughout Revelation in just a few words?
3. In Revelation, the beasts from the sea and "Babylon" are John's way of talking about the Roman Empire. Why does John depict such a close relationship between the dragon (Satan) and the beasts (13:1-18)? How do you imagine first-century Christians facing imperial persecution heard and reacted to the judgment and downfall of "Babylon" in Revelation 17–18?
4. What messages does Revelation's vision of "Babylon" have for the empires in today's world and those who live in them?

5. While Revelation discusses war between God and Satan, how does John make clear the conflict's outcome is never in doubt (12:7-12; 20:1-3, 7-10)? How can this certain outcome encourage, challenge, and motivate you and your congregation?
6. Why is there no temple in the New Jerusalem (21:22)? no sun or moon (21:23; 22:5)? no night (21:25)? nothing unclean (21:27)? How do these absences communicate the presence of God (21:3-4)?
7. The Christians for whom John wrote were a persecuted, powerless minority. How can Christians in different circumstances two thousand years later read and respond to Revelation in faithful ways?
8. What is one significant way your thinking about the Bible has changed in this year of reading it? What is one significant way how you follow Christ has changed?

Closing

- Ask for several volunteers to summarize what they have found most meaningful about your discussion or about the biblical text this week. How might God be calling them to respond to it?
- Invite the group to raise any prayer concerns or lift up any reasons for joy and thanksgiving.
- Lead the group in a short closing prayer or invite a volunteer to do so.

NOTES

1. *The New Interpreter's Study Bible* (Nashville: Abingdon, 2003), 797.
2. *New Interpreter's Study Bible*, 767.
3. *New Interpreter's Study Bible*, 918.
4. *New Interpreter's Study Bible*, 952.
5. Also because of a misconstrual of 2 Chronicles 35:25. *New Interpreter's Study Bible*, 1141.
6. *New Interpreter's Study Bible*, 1100.
7. *New Interpreter's Study Bible*, 1249-1251.
8. *New Interpreter's Study Bible*, 1985.
9. *New Interpreter's Study Bible*, 2096.
10. Morna D. Hooker, "The Letter to the Philippians," *The New Interpreter's Bible*, Vol. XI (Nashville: Abingdon Press, 2000), 527.
11. *New Interpreter's Study Bible*, 2147.